TEACHER'S GUIDE TO
Social and Emotional Learning

GRADE 4

First Printing, 2014
ISBN-13: 978-1505368451
ISBN-10: 1505368456

SMARTLYU Inc.
P.O. Box 1941
Los Altos, CA 94022

WWW.SMARTLYU.COM

DISCLAIMER:
This book is presented solely for educational purposes. You understand that this book is not intended as a substitute for consultation with a licensed medical or educational professional. While best efforts have been used in preparing this book, the author and publisher make no representations or warranties of any kind and assume no liabilities of any kind with respect to the accuracy or completeness of the contents and specifically disclaim any implied warranties of merchantability or fitness of use for a particular purpose. Neither the author nor the publisher shall be held liable or responsible to any person or entity with respect to any loss or incidental or consequential damages caused, or alleged to have been caused, directly or indirectly, by the information or programs contained herein. No warranty may be created or extended by sales representatives or written sales materials. Every school and student is different and the advice and strategies contained herein may not be suitable for your situation. You should seek the services of a competent professional before beginning any improvement program. The story and its characters and entities are fictional. Any likeness to actual persons, either living or dead, is strictly coincidental.

Table of Contents

Introduction

The SmartlyU Teacher's Guide to Social and Emotional Learning is a perfect supplement to any classroom social and emotional curriculum. It is designed for school counselors and classroom teachers. The goal of the book is to be an easily accessible resource to browse and learn about Social and Emotional competencies, and to set the framework to begin incorporating Social and Emotional teaching into the classroom.

BENEFITS OF SEL

Extensive research shows that preparing children for the real world means not just focusing on academic skills, but also incorporating important social and emotional skills into the curriculum. These life skills develop innate self-confidence and internal grit, and include skills such as recognizing one's emotions and those of others, looking at situations from different perspectives, setting goals, building positive relationships, making sound decisions, and other important SEL competencies. Giving students both the knowledge and the tools to practice these skills in their daily lives has a transformational affect. Not only does it make them happier in school, but it also makes them better learners. If children are able to manage stress, work collaboratively, and incorporate other SEL competencies, they will be able to be better focused on schoolwork.

About the SmartlyU Social and Emotional Learning Program

The SmartlyU Social and Emotional Learning program was founded by Sunita Lokuge who brings a breadth of experience as a serial entrepreneur and educator. As a cutting-edge education services company, SmartlyU offers print and web-based social and emotional learning programs for elementary and middle school children. The SmartlyU SEL programs build self-confidence, resilience, communication, and leadership skills with developmentally appropriate content. Our students are provided with opportunities to develop, showcase, and incorporate their strengths, skills, and knowledge into every aspect of their lives. The SmartlyU programs continue to transform thousands of children nationally. For more information, visit www.smartlyU.com.

How to use this book

The book outlines SEL competencies in five broad categories: Relationship Skills, Managing Emotions, Personal Development, Self-Awareness, and Organization Skills. Each competency has:

1. COMPETENCY DESCRIPTION

This section is a child counselor's take on the competency. It provides an overview of the competency and illustrates what children are going through when experiencing the competency, why the competency might be challenging for children, and how the competency can have a big impact on the child's life.

2. TEACHER STRATEGIES

Strategies are provided for teachers to use in the classroom to develop the particular competency. These strategies include helpful tips and advice for teachers so as to encourage the children and help them to grow with strong SEL competencies. These strategies also identify how teachers can get past common barriers in connecting with children and help them to find their own way.

3. PARENT STRATEGIES

Parents often ask how to develop social and emotional skills in their child. The Parent Strategies may be shared with parents to engage them in understanding how they can best work with and encourage their children. The strategies outlined in this section provide recommendations for coaching children, as well as suggestions for looking at the situation from the child's perspective.

4. CHILD STRATEGIES

Strategies are provided to impart information about the competency to children. These strategies give children practical activities to engage in, and suggestions for how to frame responses and word choices to use for stronger, healthier relationships with others. Teachers can use the Child Strategies by:

- Finding opportunities to share the children's strategies in the classroom.
- Asking students how they would use each of these strategies in various situations.

5. DISCUSSION TOPICS

The discussion topics are a great starting point to gather input on what children understand about a competency and also to generate a rich conversation. The questions enable children to develop a deeper understanding of the competency and to make use of critical thinking skills. Teachers can make use of the discussion topics by:

- Breaking the classroom up in groups of two or three children per group and offering them one of the discussion topics to explore.
- After the discussion, asking students to come up to the front of the class and share their group discussion.

6. A SAMPLE SCENARIO

The scenario is intended for children to role-play and learn key SEL concepts along the way. It incorporates a set of guided questions and provides step-by-step instructions for how to work with children in role-playing. It is highly recommended that children engage in these role-playing scenarios to help them to better understand the competency and consider various situations from different perspectives than their own, and to encourage empathy among the children.

HOW THE ROLE-PLAYING SCENARIOS WORK:

Role-playing is an active learning experience, which leads to ownership of skills that can be used in everyday life. Invite students to explore the scenarios outlined in each competency by engaging in role-playing activities:

1. Set the scene: Read the scenario out loud. Invite one student for each character in the scenario to join you at the front of the class, and assign each person a character to play. Ask the students to re-enact the scene as you have described it. *PLEASE NOTE: For scenarios that contain physical confrontation, ask students to begin the scene AFTER the moment of physical contact, or to perform the scene WITHOUT making physical contact.*

2. Facilitate an activity period: After the students have performed the scenario, you may choose to:

   a. Have a class-wide discussion and ask the questions listed after the scenario (under the heading "Guided Questions"), and encourage both the actors and the rest of the class to respond. These questions include opportunities for students to complete the scenario using both positive and negative responses, as well as opportunities for students to share their own personal experiences similar to the scenario associated with the competency.

b. Have the class split up into small groups of two to three students and assign different discussion questions to each group. The groups can discuss and share in front of the class.

c. Have students draw a cartoon inventing a similar situation and share with the class.

Relationship Skills

Breaking into Cliques

Friendship groups are a normal part of the social tapestry for both children and adults. Social connections are formed as people find others who share similar interests, values, experiences, and personalities. Other factors that influence how people make social networks are gender, age, proximity, family backgrounds, culture, and shared activities, among others. Being able to form a new friendship or enter an established group or clique can be challenging, but can offer growth opportunities for everyone involved.

It's important to keep in mind that the concept of "cliques" refers to both the valuable aspects of being part of a group as well as some of the difficulties of exclusive groups. On the one hand, cliques can provide a sense of belonging, having a supportive network, and learning social rules in order to interact with others. On the other hand, cliques can become exclusive and limiting, and often can result in mean or hurtful behaviors between the group members or with others who are not part of the clique.

Furthermore, the social tapestry is complicated since friendship groups are often shifting and challenge children to develop different skills to manage the demands within changing social dynamics. For instance, children that either move to a new school or join a new team/activity often have to cope with the anxiety associated with making new friends. As children change throughout their lives, their friendships may also change.

In and out of school, adults can model ways that children can introduce themselves either to an individual or a group. Helping a child to be open to exploring different types of friends and relating to a variety of people can facilitate new relationships and help them build social skills.

Teacher Strategies

- Create a buddy system for new students. Clearly define what the buddy's responsibility is, e.g. hang out at recess for a specific week and introduce the new student to others.

- A teacher can also approach a group of children that know each other and ask for their leadership in including a new student.

- Teaching children the importance of inclusion through story can be very powerful, as well as discussing how recess time is being experienced by all.

- Teachers can organize group activities, creating new mixes of students to include new students and avoid promoting cliques.

Child Strategies

- Make the first move – introduce yourself!

- Practice friendly behavior – smile, listen to others, share, and join conversations.

- Find common ground – a wonderful way to initiate a friendship is finding things you might share in common with another child.

- Role-play introductions in your mind.

- You may want to find one person in the group that you would like to introduce yourself to first.

- Show flexibility and adapt to the group's choice of games.

Parent Strategies

Parents might feel just as overwhelmed when their child moves schools or when their child complains that all the students are playing a game they don't like.

- Help your child learn new sports or games by watching sports on TV or getting involved in different group activities.

- Meet parents in the class and find out whether students meet at a park or how play dates are set up.

- Ask the teacher for advice on who they observe your child hanging out with at school or for their suggestions of peers so you can arrange a play date.

- Request a buddy.

- Explore a social skills group for your child if you find they may need to develop specific social skills (flexible thinking, expected vs. unexpected behaviors, communication skills, etc.).

Teacher's Guide to Social and Emotional Learning

Discussion Topics

WHAT IS A CLIQUE?

A clique is a group of friends that does not readily allow others to join them. Cliques often share common interests and identify themselves by those interests; for example, the cheerleaders, the football players, or the drama club.

IS IT POSSIBLE TO JOIN A CLIQUE?

While it can feel intimidating to break into a clique, it is important to remember that they are made up of individual people with their own personalities and interests. One way to join a clique is to join the activity that the members have in common. You might also try introducing yourself to one member of the group and initiating a friendship with that person. They, in turn, will introduce you to the rest of the group.

DISCUSSION QUESTIONS

- What are some of the cliques that you can identify in your school?

- Do you belong to a clique? If so, do you all share a common interest?

- Do you allow other people to join your clique? Why or why not?

- Do you think cliques are a good thing? Why or why not?

- Identify a circumstance in which a clique could be a bad thing.

- Do you think it is important to accept new people into your social circle? Why or why not?

Role Play

Scenario: It is the first day of school and James is at a table in class where everyone already knows each other. He is feeling left out.

Setting up the Scene: Please review the guidelines in the "How to use this book" section of the introduction.

Guided Questions: After the students have performed the scenario, ask the following questions *(invite both the actors and the rest of the class to answer)*:

DISCUSS FEELINGS:

- What is James feeling?

- What are the other children at the table feeling?

THINKING ABOUT CHOICES:

- What do you think could happen if James doesn't introduce himself or try to talk to the other kids?

- How would James benefit by not making an effort with the other kids?

- What could James say or do to get to know the other kids and break into their group?

- Do you think that by not making the effort now, James might continue to have difficulty break into groups of friends? Why?

MAKING IT PERSONAL:

Help students relate the scenario to their own lives by asking the following:

- Has a situation like this ever happened to you? What did you do?

- Is it easier to try to make friends or to keep to yourself in this type of situation? Why?

- What kinds of things do you think or say to yourself to help you feel confident and break into cliques?

- What are other situations similar to this where you've had to make new friends or approach kids who already know each other? What happened?

Teacher's Guide to Social and Emotional Learning

Conflict Resolution

A conflict is a disagreement between parties. Conflicts are a normal part of life, which is why conflict resolution is an essential life skill that develops over time. Both children and adults encounter different types and levels of conflict daily and learn how to cope and work through them by adopting, expanding, and refining their own repertoire of strategies. Conflict provides opportunities to expand and weave together skills and qualities such as empathy, negotiation, resilience, and emotional intelligence, amongst others.

Conflict resolution teaches children that there are peaceful solutions to disagreements. Children who don't learn conflict resolution techniques often resort to violence and struggle to control strong feelings. Conflict resolution calls upon many skills such as employing techniques for calming down, listening skills, effective communication, and negotiating. Through role-playing and practice, children can learn that by employing a process to resolve conflicts, the conflicts themselves don't need to be avoided. Through practice, children get empowered to find their voice.

23

Teacher Strategies

- Talk to the children about different types of conflict and have them share or role-play the types of conflicts they are facing.

- Find and provide guidance or training to a mediator to be the neutral party when resolving conflict.

- Stress that conflicts can be resolved.

- Support and coach children when they need to work out conflict issues by helping them say what they feel, listen to each other, and come up with possible solutions to address their needs and feelings.

Child Strategies

- When you are in a conflict situation, first find ways to calm strong feelings.

- Listen to the issue at hand; through listening, you will automatically help the other party calm down.

- Find areas of agreement.

- Through negotiation and compromise, find possible solutions.

- Agree on a solution that is not one-sided.

- If you are unable to find a solution that works, seek the help of an adult.

Parent Strategies

- Listen and share ideas on how children could work through a conflict, such as taking turns, finding common ground, compromising, talking out loud, etc.

- Help your child identify their personal triggers to have a better response and manage their emotions more effectively.

- Share your own stories and ways in which you resolve conflict at home and at work.

- Remind your child how it feels to not have their opinion count.

- Give your child an opportunity to practice persuasion techniques.

- Help your child keep a flexible stance or view by helping them brainstorm different ways to look at the situation or a variety of options to address it, and give praise when they keep an open perspective.

Discussion Topics

WHAT IS CONFLICT?

A conflict is a disagreement between two parties. Conflicts are a normal part of life, which is why knowing how to deal with them in a calm and clear-headed manner is an important skill. Techniques for calming down, listening skills, effective communication, and negotiation are all appropriate ways to deal with conflict.

WHY IS IT IMPORTANT TO SOLVE CONFLICTS IN A CALM MANNER?

People who do not learn calm and fair ways to solve problems often resort to violence and can have trouble controlling their strong feelings. Because of this, they have difficulty working with others and struggle to develop positive relationships. Conflicts cannot always be avoided. In fact, many conflicts arise from issues that need to be resolved for the well-being of those involved. Therefore, it is important to know how to resolve them effectively when they occur.

DISCUSSION QUESTIONS

- How do you help yourself stay calm in a conflict situation?

- Why is listening to the other side an important step in conflict resolution?

- How can negotiation be used to resolve conflicts?

- Share a time when you used negotiation to resolve a conflict.

- What are some communication skills used during conflict resolution?

- Have you ever witnessed or experienced a time when people did not take steps to resolve a conflict in a calm manner? What happened? How could the conflict have been resolved differently?

Role Play

Scenario: Samantha is new in the neighborhood and she is asked by a group of girls to join them. They are playing a game Samantha does not know.

Setting up the Scene: Please review the guidelines in the "How to use this book" section of the introduction.

Guided Questions: After the students have performed the scenario, ask the following questions *(invite both the actors and the rest of the class to answer)*:

DISCUSS FEELINGS:

- What is Samantha feeling?

- What are the group of girls feeling?

THINKING ABOUT CHOICES:

- What do you think could happen if Samantha tells the girls that they must play a game she knows or she won't join their game?

- What benefits would Samantha get from choosing not to play with these girls unless she gets her way?

- How could Samantha play with the group of girls if she does not know the game they are playing?

- Do you think it might become a habit for Samantha to not be flexible when she does not know the game a group of children are playing? Why?

- What could happen if it became a habit?

MAKING IT PERSONAL:

Help students relate the scenario to their own lives by asking the following:

- Has a situation like this ever happened to you? What did you do?

- Is it easier to tell other people that they should play a game you know, or for you to try the game they are playing? Why?

- What kinds of things do you think or say to yourself to help you make good choices in a situation like this?

- What are other situations similar to this where it was really hard to make a good choice (for example, when you have to figure out a fair way to fix an issue)?

Coping with Crushes

As children get older, they begin to experience new and more complex emotions, which can be confusing and overwhelming at times since they are not sure how to handle them yet. One of these feelings is having their first heart-throbbing and exciting crush. Crushes are a natural and positive emotion, a precursor to feelings of love and learning how to handle heartbreak. As a new awareness of gender begins to emerge, so do crushes. For most children, their first crush may happen around fifth or sixth grade, but, for some kids, it could be as early as second grade.

Due to the novelty of this feeling, the child often feels awkward, shy, and inexperienced as to what to do. He may daydream about the person and feel happy, nervous, and excited at the same time. A child may choose to do silly behaviors that are uncharacteristic of them, like chasing the person they like around school, giving them notes, calling or texting them, or teasing them to get attention. Friends might share the buzz, and with it might come the gossip and the ups and downs of handling this new experience. As the young ones are deeply tangled in the myriad of emotions, it is interesting to take a removed perspective and to understand that a crush is a projection of idealized characteristics, hopes, desires, and fantasies, and thus a creation of a platonic image bestowed on someone else. In other words, the crush has to do much more with the person feeling it than with whom the admired one is. This is why a child can have a crush on someone they know (a friend, a classmate, etc.) or someone they have never even met, like a celebrity.

Crushes are often temporary and fade as the magical thinking and idealization tend to shift. However, while they last, crushes are felt intensely and thus parents need to take them seriously and support their child through them. In particular, with new social media venues (email, Snapchat, Facebook, etc.), crushes can move at a faster pace and may also bring consequences that are difficult to handle (for instance, online gossip or an insensitive response seen by many viewers), which is why it is so important to have an adult to help the child sort out this feeling in a new stage.

Teacher Strategies

- If a student shares he/she has a crush, handle it with care, not taking it lightly or joking about it, since crushes feels very real to the child.

- Be the calm voice so as to not add to the excitement or promote the buzz around the crush.

- Remind students that crushes are normal and positive even through their ups and downs, yet if someone is feeling uncomfortable about the crush or there is a red flag (such as obsessive thinking), then talk to the children involved.

- Address gossip and teasing and remind kids that rules of behavior still apply.

Child Strategies

- Find a creative way to express your emotions, such as journaling, doing art work, or writing songs or poems (even if you decide to not share them with anyone).

- Talk to someone you trust about how you feel – your parents, teachers, or school counselor can help in sorting through your feelings and brainstorm ideas of what you can do.

- If you decide to tell a friend, keep in mind that other people could find out and think of how you may want to respond if others know.

- You may choose to act as normal as possible around the person you like or share with them how you feel, but it is important you do not tease them or make them feel uncomfortable.

- If the other person likes you back it can be a great feeling, but if they don't share the same feeling, you might feel sad, hurt, and embarrassed. Talk to someone who can be there to support you through this sadness and know that this heartbreak will go away in time.

- If someone likes you, and you do not feel the same way back, try to tell them in a kind way.

Parent Strategies

- Be there to listen to your child if they share they have a crush and handle it with care.

- Follow their lead; if they are acting silly you can parallel with humor or excitement, but if they share with a serious tone correspond with a serious response.

- Talking to your child about your first crush can normalize and validate the feeling.

- While giving them space if they are not ready to share yet, help facilitate a reflection with the following questions:

  - What might they want to do about a crush? Keep it to themselves or not?
  - What might happen if other people find out?
  - What if the other person does not like them back in the same way? Could they keep the relationship friendly?

- Talk to your child about how they can show their feeling without making someone uncomfortable – for instance, instead of teasing someone, giving that person a compliment.

- If someone has a crush on them and they do not like them back, talk about how they could respond in a kind way.

Discussion Topics

WHAT IS A CRUSH?

A crush is a word used to describe strong feelings of attraction for another person. A person experiencing a crush might find themselves thinking about and wanting to spend time with someone in particular, but may feel shy and embarrassed when they are actually around them. A crush is a little bit like romantic love between adults, and the crushes you have when you are young help you to figure out the characteristics you will be looking for in a romantic relationship when you get older.

SHOULD YOU SHARE YOUR FEELINGS?

Experiencing a crush for the first time can feel confusing. It's important to find someone to talk to about what you are feeling. A trusted adult like a parent, teacher, or school counselor can help you sort through your thoughts and emotions. You may choose to talk to a close friend, but keep in mind that there is always a chance that other people could find out. Think about how you would respond if other people knew about your feelings. You may even choose to tell the person that you have a crush on, and there is always a chance they will feel the same way about you. If they don't share the same feelings, you might feel sad, hurt, and embarrassed. In this case, it is important to talk about your feelings of sadness with someone you trust.

38

DISCUSSION QUESTIONS

- What are some creative ways to express the feelings of a crush? You may or may not share these expressions with other people (examples: journaling, artwork, etc.).

- What would you do if a friend told you that they had a crush on someone?

- What would you do if someone told you that they had a crush on you, but you don't feel the same way about them?

- Why is it important not to tease or gossip about people who have shared that they have a crush on someone?

Teacher's Guide to Social and Emotional Learning

Role Play

Scenario: Cora has a crush on Ryan, and her friends found out about it when she was doodling his name in her notebook during class.

Setting up the Scene: Please review the guidelines in the "How to use this book" section of the introduction.

Guided Questions: After the students have performed the scenario, ask the following questions *(invite both the actors and the rest of the class to answer)*:

DISCUSS FEELINGS:

- What is Cora feeling?

- What are Cora's friends feeling?

THINKING ABOUT CHOICES:

- What do you think could happen if Cora laughs and pretends it's just a joke?

- What would Cora gain by not telling her friends the truth?

- What can Cora do to best handle her crush?

- Do you think Cora should talk to her friends about how she feels or just pretend it never happened? Why?

- Do you think it could become a habit for Cora to get carried away by her feelings? What could happen if it becomes a habit?

MAKING IT PERSONAL:

Help students relate the scenario to their own lives by asking the following:

- Has a situation like this ever happened to you? What did you do?

- Is it easier to talk to your friends about your feelings around crushes, or not? Why?

- What kinds of things do you think or say to yourself to help deal with a crush?

- What are other situations similar to this where it was really hard to make a good choice (such as talking to your friends about your crush or dealing with situations that might feel embarrassing)?

Dealing with Different Personalities

A friend can be a source of self-esteem, affection, encouragement, and enjoyment. We know the importance of having close, lasting, and genuine relationships to fulfill and enhance our social and emotional lives. As we grow and develop meaningful connections, we realize the qualities that are important to us in friends, such as honesty, loyalty, trustworthiness, sense of humor, being a good listener, etc. However, we also realize that rarely does the course of childhood friendships run smoothly and that actually these unavoidable social missteps teach us the social skills and coping mechanisms that will help us solidify our good friendships.

One of these common and difficult learning points is the imbalance in a relationship when one child has a strong character and can be dominating, while the other child does not know how to use their voice and feels ineffective in setting their own limits. Adults can help coach both children to find a better balance and thus strengthen what could be a positive relationship.

Teacher's Guide to Social and Emotional Learning

To help both children in this specific situation, it is essential to learn the skill of assertive communication. It is quite possible that their communication style so far is more aggressive and passive. Lisa M. Schab, LCSW, author of *Cool, Calm and Confident: A Workbook to Help Kids Learn Assertiveness Skills*, defines assertiveness as the "healthiest style of communication. Assertiveness involves recognizing and standing up for our own rights, while at the same time recognizing and respecting the rights of others." Therefore, in order to be assertive, both children need to be empathetic and, at the same time, voice what they want and need in a kind yet clear way.

Teacher Strategies

- Facilitate a dialogue supporting the children to use their voices and to listen to reach a win-win balanced situation for both. Each child might need to be coached before they can sit down together, so that each one is ready to listen and say what they need.

- Pair children up in classwork so that there is a balance of their personalities.

- Have the children journal with topic questions that help them clarify what is important to them, what they like, who they are, etc. in order to build their self-awareness and confidence.

- Introduce the concept of different styles of communication: aggressive, passive, and assertive. Role-play and analyze these responses so that the children can practice being in an assertive role (help them look at tone, body language, and content).

Child Strategies

If you feel your friend is being bossy:

- Talk to your friend about how you feel using "I" statements, like, "I feel you do not listen to me a lot of the time."

- Think of what you want or need them to do. For example, look at your friend and in a clear and strong tone say, "I want to suggest an idea of what we can play today."

- Practice with your parents, siblings, and teacher on how to say things in a way that is strong.

- Keep in mind that in the beginning your friend might get angry because they are not used to you using your voice, but if he or she is a good friend, they will work to make you feel better.

If friends tell you that you are bossy:

- Listen to your friend's feelings and needs and repeat to them what you hear. For example, "You feel like I am not listening and want to play outside instead."

- Take turns and make sure all of you have a chance to make decisions: "OK, let's try your idea," or, "What character do you want to be today in our game?"

- Look at your friend's face and body language. Do they look like they are having a good time or are they getting upset?

- Ask your friends how they are feeling and if they are OK with your suggestions.

Parent Strategies

When your child is the dominating friend:

- Teach your child to compromise and be flexible by helping them negotiate what they want with siblings and friends to try to reach a win-win situation.

- Help your child pay attention to their tone, and, if it sounds bossy, model and practice different ways of saying things.

- Help them develop active listening by asking them to repeat or summarize what the other person is saying.

- Help them read body language and detect what someone might be feeling.

- Play games and guide your child by complimenting when they are playing well, and make suggestions when you see their interactions are overpowering and inflexible.

When your child is taking a passive role:

- Help your child find their voice by practicing words they can then use in different scenarios, like, "I feel like we usually play what you want; let's try my idea today."

- Help them identify and advocate for their feelings, wants, and needs.

- Role-play and model the body language they can use to be assertive (standing tall, looking eye to eye, having a calm but clear tone, etc.).

- Brainstorm with your child things they would like to suggest in games or projects and tell them that it is OK to express those ideas and stand up to others.

- If your child often gives in quickly to friends and siblings, support them in sticking to their decisions and being more assertive.

- Help your child write down what they would like to say to a friend in a kind but assertive way, and then read it out loud and practice how they would say it.

Discussion Topics

WHAT ARE PERSONALITY TRAITS?

Personality traits are the characteristics that make people different from one another. While friends often have interests in common, they do not always have the same type of personality. For example, one friend may be shy while the other is more assertive. In a relationship like this, it is important to find balance, so that the more assertive friend does not make all of the decisions. After all, a healthy relationship is one in which both members' needs are being met.

WHAT DOES A BALANCED FRIENDSHIP LOOK LIKE?

A balanced friendship is one in which both people have their voices heard. It is important for shy individuals to use assertive language to speak up for themselves; for example, offering suggestions as to what activities they would like to do. It is important for the more assertive person in a friendship to be a good listener and to make an effort to allow the shy friend to make some decisions.

Teacher's Guide to Social and Emotional Learning

DISCUSSION QUESTIONS

- Have you ever spoken up to a bossy friend? What did you say?

- What should you do if your friend tells you that you are too bossy?

- Would you describe yourself as shy or assertive? Why?

- How can you let a friend know that you are listening when they share their feelings with you?

- What are some ways to make sure that both members of a friendship get a chance to make decisions?

Role Play

Scenario: Grace feels that Audrey bosses everyone around in all the games they play. Today, Audrey is deciding who gets what role in the "school game," and Grace does not like being assigned to be the "bad kid" in class again.

Setting up the Scene: Please review the guidelines in the "How to use this book" section of the introduction.

Guided Questions: After the students have performed the scenario, ask the following questions *(invite both the actors and the rest of the class to answer)*:

DISCUSS FEELINGS:

- What is Grace feeling?

- What is Audrey feeling?

THINKING ABOUT CHOICES:

- What do you think could happen if Grace starts bossing Audrey around in return?

- How would it benefit Grace to be bossy to Audrey?

- How could Grace handle this situation so that it's fair for everyone?

- Do you think that it could become a habit for Grace to be bossy to others? Why?

52

MAKING IT PERSONAL:

Help students relate the scenario to their own lives by asking the following:

- Has a situation like this ever happened to you? What did you do?

- In a situation like this, would it be easier to be bossy to your friend to see how they like it, or to calmly talk to them about how you feel? Why?

- What kinds of things do you think or say to yourself to help you make a good choice when you're dealing with someone who has a different personality than yours?

- What are other situations like this where it was really hard to make a good choice (for example, dealing with someone who is bossy or does things differently than you do)?

DEALING WITH DIFFERENT PERSONALITIES

54

Dealing with Exclusion

Part of healthy human development lies in our need, desire, and ability to connect to others and to belong. Being part of a group helps us develop our identity, our values, and our views of the world, as well as our sense of self. What is more, recognized psychologist Maslow's (1943, 1954) hierarchy of needs placed "the need to belong" as one of the most important basic human needs after physiological and safety needs. It is therefore understandable that one of the hardest things to cope with is exclusion.

Although difficult, there will probably be a time when a child has to cope with some type of exclusion as friendship patterns shift, children experiment with their allegiances, and they try to figure out social dynamics. These types of challenges are part of learning and building resilience, self-esteem, and confidence, especially with the caring support from their family, friends, and teachers. Exclusionary behavior, often used by cliques to exclude peers, uses phrases like, "This table is full," "You can't join us now," and "We don't like your game."

Teacher's Guide to Social and Emotional Learning

Teacher Strategies

- Read books about inclusion/exclusion and have a class discussion about why people may exclude others, and how each child might feel in the situation.

- Discuss how everyone feels in the group, and remind them that as a class the expectations are to include others.

- Rotate kids in tables and in projects to offer different opportunities to create new connections.

- Select a group of kids to join you for lunch (a mixed group of kids with strong and weak social skills), and ask them to invite a friend. Make it fun and special and plan "get to know you" activities, while facilitating conversations by modeling social skills.

- Find a strong, positive, and grounded student who may serve as a voice to help others include a student in games or activities.

If you see exclusionary behavior, bring the group of children together and talk about the issue:

- Let them know that you will be monitoring the situation.

- Monitor lunchtime activity.

- Meet with the parent of the child that is practicing such behavior.

Child Strategies

- Include others in your games (especially if you see they look like they are feeling alone) by inviting them to join or asking for their suggestions, or by saying, "Do you want to join us?"

- If you are not able to join a game or a group, look for other alternatives – keep your options open.

- Be open to making different friends that you may initially not consider close or similar to you.

- Say hello and ask to join a game.

- Share your feelings with others, for instance by saying, "I felt hurt when you said I could not play with you. What would make me feel better is if I can join you."

- Speak to your teacher or school counselor if you feel you have tried different things and they are not working.

Parent Strategies

- As a family, teach empathy and model respect for diversity and valuing inclusion.

- Talk and actively listen to your child as they share the ups and downs of their friendships.

- If your child does not usually share much about their friendships, look out for signs that your child may be feeling distressed; for example, if they do not want to go to school, they do not speak about any friends, or they are irritable or angry.

- If your child shares a specific situation of exclusion, keep your feelings in check and try to get a sense of different perspectives, what may have happened, and how long it has been going on.

- If you feel this needs to be addressed further, talk to the teacher, coach, or school counselor and ask whether they have noticed a problem. Then, work with them to brainstorm ideas on how to support your child.

- Try to determine whether your child may be excluded because of their behavior and if they therefore need support with social skills.

- Ensure your child has opportunities to get to know children in different scenarios, for instance in after-school activities.

- Create a script and role-play how your child can join a group.

Discussion Topics

WHAT IS EXCLUSION?

Exclusion, or the feeling of being excluded, happens when a person feels that they are being left out of a group. A sense of belonging is the feeling that you are accepted and have a place within your family, friends, and community. We all feel the need to belong, so feeling excluded is a hurtful situation to be in.

WHEN DOES EXCLUSION HAPPEN?

Exclusion happens any time a group does not accept someone. An example might be a group of friends purposefully leaving someone out of an activity or refusing to let someone sit with them at lunch. Sometimes people feel excluded because they are too shy to ask to be included. They may assume that others will not let them join even if that is not the case.

DISCUSSION QUESTIONS

- Share a time when you felt excluded from a group.

- What can you say if you see a group or activity that you want to join?

- What can you do if you see someone being left out of an activity?

- Who can you talk to if you are feeling left out?

- What advice would you give to a friend who is feeling left out?

- If a group repeatedly leaves you out and treats you poorly, should you continue to try to join them? Why or why not?

Role Play

Scenario: Jordyn is a new student in Katherine's class and she seems really nice, but one of Katherine's friends has told her not to talk to Jordyn.

Setting up the Scene: Please review the guidelines in the "How to use this book" section of the introduction.

Guided Questions: After the students have performed the scenario, ask the following questions *(invite both the actors and the rest of the class to answer)*:

DISCUSS FEELINGS:

- What is Katherine feeling?

- What is Jordyn feeling?

THINKING ABOUT CHOICES:

- What do you think could happen if Katherine listens to her friend so that she does not get mad, and excludes Jordyn?

- What could Katherine gain by not hanging out with Jordyn?

- How could Katherine try to be friends with both her old friend and Jordyn?

- Do you think that it could become a habit for Katherine to exclude others whenever her friends tell her to? What could happen if it becomes a habit?

62

MAKING IT PERSONAL:

Help students relate the scenario to their own lives by asking the following:

- Has a situation like this ever happened to you? What did you do?

- In a situation like this, would it be easier to not make friends with the new student or be friends with the new student when your other friend isn't paying attention, or to calmly talk to your friends about how you feel? Why?

- What kinds of things do you think or say to yourself to help you make a good choice when people are being excluded?

- What are other situations similar to this where it was really hard to make a good choice (for example, if you see someone being excluded)?

Teacher's Guide to Social and Emotional Learning

Friendship Skills

During childhood and adolescence in particular, friendships and peer acceptance are very important factors in development and psychological adjustment. Friends provide a connection with reality and serve as a valuable support system. The array of social interactions is vast; where one child may prefer to have one close friend, another child may choose to move freely between friendship groups and have a variety of connections. Research has shown that having healthy relationships during this time is crucial, and being isolated can affect a child or youth's self-image and self-esteem, creating feelings of incompetence, inadequacy, and loneliness, resulting in a variety of behavioral problems.

It is important to note that technology is now intricately woven into our social tapestry – especially when it comes to the social tapestry of today's youth. In this new backdrop, the meaning of friendship takes on new shades. However, experts remind us that, in the end, the essence and importance of close connections remains the same.

Teacher Strategies

- Reward behaviors – create "Friendship Cards" which have positive words and phrases on them, such as, "Love your smile," "Thanks for sharing," "Thanks for standing up for your friends," and "Flexible," and hand these out to children as they exhibit these positive behaviors.

- Discuss how and when students should work out their issues with others rather than asking adults to fix all of their problems. Introduce the idea of big problems that adults should know about and problems that they can work out on their own to help them to better understand.

- Teach children how to recognize body language of others.

Child Strategies

- Talk to friends and find out about shared interests that you have in common.

- Listen – when someone is speaking to you, listen to them and wait for your turn to respond to what they say.

- Join in games that you want to play in.

- Compliment your friends when they do well.

- Build trust – when you tell your friend you will do something, follow through with your promise and do it.

FRIENDSHIP SKILLS

Teacher's Guide to Social and Emotional Learning

Parent Strategies

- Find opportunities to point out friendly behavior that you exhibit at the bank, grocery store, etc.

  - Ask your child how that made the other person feel.

  - Discuss how it made you feel.

- Teach sharing among siblings or friends.

- Share the qualities of good friendships such as having fun with your friend, being able to share ideas freely, listening and standing up for each other.

- Help your child to think before they talk. Words spoken without thought can hurt others.

- Talk about things that should not be done in friendship such as hurtful teasing, gossiping, bragging, dominating a friend, etc.

- Show children how they can give compliments and praise their friends; for example, praise a friend on something they do well.

- Explain that friendships can have ups and downs. You may not always agree with everything your friend has to say and that is OK. Each of us can have our own opinions and still be friends.

Discussion Topics

WHAT IS FRIENDSHIP?

Friendship is a relationship between people who enjoy spending time with one another. Often, they share common interests and spend time enjoying these interests together. Friends trust one another, are comfortable being themselves together, and can share their feelings and ideas without fear of being judged. Even when they disagree, friends are able to resolve their differences.

WHY IS IT IMPORTANT TO HAVE FRIENDS?

In addition to having fun together, friends provide a support system. They can help you feel brave as you face your fears, give advice when you are making tough decisions, and help you learn new skills. Friends want the best for one another and help each other reach goals.

FRIENDSHIP SKILLS

DISCUSSION QUESTIONS

- What are some common interests that you share with your friends?

- Share a time when a friend helped you during a difficult situation.

- Share a time when you had a disagreement with a friend. How did you resolve your problem?

- How can you build trust in a friendship?

- What can you do if you hurt a friend's feelings?

- Do friends always get along?

- What is your favorite aspect of having friends?

Role Play

Scenario: Caleb notices that everyone is playing with someone at recess and he is all alone.

Setting up the Scene: Please review the guidelines in the "How to use this book" section of the introduction.

Guided Questions: After the students have performed the scenario, ask the following questions *(invite both the actors and the rest of the class to answer)*:

DISCUSS FEELINGS:

- What is Caleb feeling?

- What are the other children at recess feeling?

Teacher's Guide to Social and Emotional Learning

THINKING ABOUT CHOICES:

- What do you think could happen if Caleb doesn't try to play with the other kids?

- What benefits would Caleb get from waiting for someone else to come to him and invite him to play?

- What could Caleb do to get to know the other kids and play with them?

- Do you think that it could become a habit for Caleb to always wait for someone to come to him? What could happen?

MAKING IT PERSONAL:

Help students relate the scenario to their own lives by asking the following:

- Has a situation like this ever happened to you? What did you do?

- In a situation like this, would it be easier to wait for someone else to start talking, or to go to the other kids and ask if you can play with them? Why?

- What kinds of things do you think or say to yourself to help you make a good choice in a situation like this?

- What are other situations like this where it was really hard to connect with others or develop your friendship skills (for example, talking to people you don't know, or trying to make new friends)?

74

Initiating Friendship

Having friends is important at every stage in life. Through time, our relationships change and fulfill different emotional needs, enriching our lives in a variety of ways. In particular, during childhood, friendships are part of healthy development as they help children learn social skills and how to communicate, solve problems, and negotiate situations that arise. In their connections, children experience an array of emotions and learn how to regulate their feelings as part of interacting with others. As friendships become more intricate and gain depth, our connections foster a sense of belonging, help us cope with difficult times, provide us with company, and help us remain flexible in the necessary give-and-take of relationships.

Making connections is something we begin to do since birth as we start giving shape to our social skills through early interactions. For some children this is an intuitive process, while others need further guidance in forming their social thinking and abilities. Research has shown that the inner workings of human relations involve sophisticated social skills in order to initiate and form mutually enjoyable connections.

For instance, initiating friendships in itself requires the ability to intuitively choose prospective friends based on reading who may share similar traits and interests, as well as who is trustworthy and reliable. A child also may inadvertently assess how different children treat others, how they make him or her feel, and who may share similar expectations of a friendship. In addition, the child needs then to initiate conversation and have the ability to relate to others in a way that he or she is liked. Thus, initiating an interaction is not a simple process, and yet it is important as it is the beginning to forming enduring relationships. Parents, educators, and mental health professionals can help provide nurturing environments and support children to have a good head start into this intricate social world.

Teacher Strategies

- Teach children how to make "people files" – guide the student to think about the kids they know, pick one, and think about some characteristics they notice about this girl or boy: what does he or she like, is he/she friendly to others, does she/he have pets, and what are his or her passions and values?

- Facilitate activities, role-plays, and discussions that help kids read body language. Help them notice what the other person's non-verbal language is saying in their interaction: is the other person smiling and continuing the conversation, are they rolling their eyes, are they being friendly, do they show interest?

- Organize buddy lunches – to help start new contacts, have kids invite a buddy they may want to get to know better to a recess lunch and help guide interactions modeling conversation starters and dialogue.

- Read books on friendships – there are wonderful books for different ages about friendships.

- Help with joining play graciously – coach kids through role-play on how to join a game, practicing the words they can use.

Child Strategies

- Choose someone – think of whom you would like to meet and feel could be a possible friend.

- Introduce yourself – come up to someone, smile, and say, "Hey! I'm _____. What's your name?" or, "Hi I'm _____. Do you want to go play ball?"

- Join play – if you see others playing, ask, "Can I join you? This looks fun."

- Offer sincere compliments – you can start a conversation with a nice compliment like, "You are really good at playing basketball; do you play in a team?" or, "I really like your book bag. What class do you have next?"

- Find similarities and interests – find people who share similar interests or passions to you so you have some common ground.

- Ask about the others and listen – show your interest by asking questions about the other person and listen to what they share without interrupting.

- Remember that friendships take time – you may take some time to get to know someone and feel close to them.

Parent Strategies

- Provide social opportunities to get to know other kids. Plan play dates with different kids (teachers may give you some possible suggestions on who would be a good option) and sign up your child to participate in extracurricular activities to get to know different people.

- Help your child become familiar with games and sports – children learn a lot about social rules and interactions through play. At home, you can play board games and teach them some basic things about sports so that they can then feel more confident to jump into a variety of games at school and other venues.

- Practice some basic skills – role play with your child on how they can smile and the words to say when approaching a new child.

- Let them work out conflicts. It is normal for conflicts to arise even during first encounters as children figure out the rules of the games or what each one wants. Let the kids try to come up with a solution and only intervene if they really are having a hard time working it out.

- Remind them to be flexible. Work with your child to let go of a rigid idea or expectation and adapt when challenges may arise. Keeping a "flexible brain" can help them to come up with other solutions and work things out.

INITIATING FRIENDSHIP

Discussion Topics

WHAT DOES IT MEAN TO INITIATE A FRIENDSHIP?

Initiating a friendship means to choose someone who you feel would make a good friend and take steps toward building a relationship with them by introducing yourself and sharing some personal information; for example, your likes and dislikes.

WHY DO YOU NEED TO KNOW HOW TO INITIATE FRIENDSHIPS?

Knowing how to start a friendship is an important social skill that you will use throughout your life. Being able to identify and introduce yourself to a potential friend means that you will be able to surround yourself with people whose company you enjoy, who share your common interests, and who are likely to share the same values. These are the foundations of a strong and lasting friendship.

80

DISCUSSION QUESTIONS

- Share a time when you made a new friend.

- What is an example of a way to introduce yourself to someone new?

- Why does having common interests help form friendships?

- Why is it important to be a good listener when talking to a new friend?

- Identify someone who you feel acts with integrity. What is the one thing you admire most about this person?

- Are strong friendships formed in a day, or do they take time? Why?

Role Play

Scenario: Avery has moved to a new school and feels like she has no friends.

Setting up the Scene: Please review the guidelines in the "How to use this book" section of the introduction.

Guided Questions: After the students have performed the scenario, ask the following questions *(invite both the actors and the rest of the class to answer)*:

DISCUSS FEELINGS:

• What is Avery feeling?

• What are the other children at the new school feeling?

THINKING ABOUT CHOICES:

• What do you think could happen if Avery worries she will never make any new friends?

• What could Avery gain by thinking that maybe the kids at this school aren't very nice?

• What are some ways that Avery could go to the other kids and try to make friends?

• Do you think that it could become a habit for Avery to not try to make new friends when she is at new places? Why?

82

MAKING IT PERSONAL:

Help students relate the scenario to their own lives by asking the following:

- Has a situation like this ever happened to you? What did you do?

- In a situation like this, would it be easier to keep to yourself, or to find something in common with a couple students and start a conversation with them? Why?

- What kinds of things do you think or say to yourself to help you make a good choice in a situation like this?

- What are other situations like this where it was really hard to make a good choice (for example, if you feel uncomfortable in a new place with people you don't know)?

84

Navigating the Social Scene

We are social beings who are constantly moving within a social world. Starting at a young age, we begin to learn how to read the social environments we are a part of and figure out how to respond based on the set of social rules that exist. As our social contexts become more complex, our social skills need to continue to develop in order to navigate the shifting social scenes we encounter. For instance, when a child starts a new grade with different teachers and peers, attends a first school party, or enters a new developmental stage like the "tween" or teenage years, the child will encounter new behavioral expectations, which will require a shift in his or her social awareness as well as the ability to decipher more sophisticated and novel ground rules.

In order to understand how social dynamics work, a child integrates multiple skills. For instance, when entering a new situation, the child needs to read what some of the social expectations are (for example, knowing what questions can be asked and which can't when meeting someone for the first time); recognize

85

subtle and non-verbal social rules (such as how he/she needs to sit down when entering a classroom if the teacher is waiting to start the class); read body language and facial expressions; grasp the meaning of a sentence based on tone and context; understand roles and relationships amongst a group of people; and interpret other people's emotions and perspectives with accuracy.

For some, social cognition comes naturally and intuitively, while for others some of the difficulties with reading social cues or understanding social nuances suggest they may need further strategies to be able to move within different social contexts in an appropriate way.

Teacher Strategies

- Introduce concepts of "Social Thinking" (Michelle Garcia Winner, 2000) and related child-centric products such as "Social Detectives," "Expected vs. unexpected behaviors," and "Superflex and the Team of Unthinkables" to your class (Winner, Michelle Garcia, and Stephanie Madrigal, 2008). Note: although these concepts originated from working with children with social learning differences, these are several concepts that can be very helpful when working with any child to support social skills.

- Create moments of Social Reflection. Help children develop social skills and understand social environments by making these obvious; in other words, stop your class in the middle of a situation and ask the kids to analyze people's body language, some of the expected behaviors at that moment, and the tone people are using.

- Support kids who may need it – if you find there is a child who may need more support to develop social skills, talk to his or her parents and come up with possible strategies and resources.

Child Strategies

- Read between the lines. We communicate not only with words, but also through body language and tone (the way we say things). Practice reading people's body language by watching their facial expressions, eyes, and how they move their hands, to figure out if they are nervous, angry, excited, etc. Reflect on whether their tone sounds like they are joking, serious, silly, etc. and respond based on this.

- If you are with friends and are confused about what is going on (for example, people are angry at each other and you do not know why), ask a friend so that you know how to respond to the situation.

- Think about what the expected behaviors are in a situation and avoid doing unexpected behaviors. For example, when doing group work, telling others in your group how they don't know anything about the project and you can do it on your own would be unexpected and will not make a good impression.

- Be flexible. When dealing with others, plans might change, people might have different feelings, disagreements can come up, and communication can be unclear. If you remain flexible you have a better chance to work it out and find a good solution.

88

Parent Strategies

- Talking to your kids about the importance of social skills is a good way to start making these abilities part of your daily life. Practice skills with your kids, like how to take turns, ask for help, learn to give compliments, use people's names when speaking to them, follow directions, be a good sport, speak up in class, or read people's body language.

- Pick one skill you feel your child needs to work on and focus on that one for a period of time. As your child feels more confident, you can work on a different skill.

- Once you and your child choose a skill to work on, define the skill (what it would look and sound like). For instance, if you want your child to ask questions or participate in class, help her think of how she would get the teacher's attention and the tone of voice she would use. Then come up with a goal (ask one question a day), help her build some tools (brainstorm questions she could ask based on what they are learning and practice words she could use), and create a chart to mark her daily progress. You may need to work with a teacher to monitor improvement and celebrate successes along the way.

- As social challenges come up, work with your child to problem-solve and explore solutions and perspectives. Working through difficulties will promote resilience toward social setbacks.

Discussion Topics

WHAT IS THE "SOCIAL SCENE"?

The "social scene" is a phrase that refers to the social environment around you, including the people and location. Navigating a social scene means knowing how to behave based on what you see, hear, and feel. Different social situations call for different behaviors; for example, you would behave differently in a library than you would at a party. Your behavior in a social scene is also affected by the people there; for example, you would behave differently on the playground with friends than you would if you were attending a dinner party with your parent's friends.

ARE THERE RULES TO FOLLOW?

Successfully navigating a social scene means paying attention to and reading the environment. The information you receive from paying attention is essentially the rules for that given social scene. Whether you are joining a group of friends who are chatting or working in a group project, take a moment to notice what people are doing and what their conversation is about, then try to blend in by adapting to what people are doing around you. It can also be helpful to pay attention to and try to match body language.

DISCUSSION QUESTIONS

- Identify two social settings in which your behavior is very different.

- Have you ever felt out of place in a social setting? What made you feel this way?

- Have you ever noticed someone who seemed out of place in a social setting? Without giving names, describe the behaviors that seemed inappropriate.

- Why is it important to pay attention to people's body language?

- Who can you ask for help if you are having trouble understanding the expectations in a social setting?

Teacher's Guide to Social and Emotional Learning

Role Play

Scenario: Ashton's friend Tommy always says he has seen the movie or played the video game when they are talking about new things. Ashton thinks he is lying.

Setting up the Scene: Please review the guidelines in the "How to use this book" section of the introduction.

Guided Questions: After the students have performed the scenario, ask the following questions *(invite both the actors and the rest of the class to answer)*:

DISCUSS FEELINGS:

- What is Ashton feeling?

- What is Tommy feeling?

THINKING ABOUT CHOICES:

- What do you think could happen if Ashton tries testing his friend, making up the name of a movie and laughing when Tommy lies and says he has seen it?

- How would it benefit Ashton to test Tommy?

- What could Ashton say to Tommy to let him know that he should not lie to his friends?

- Do you think it could become a habit for Ashton to laugh

92

at people when he catches them in a lie? What could happen?

MAKING IT PERSONAL:

Help students relate the scenario to their own lives by asking the following:

- Has a situation like this ever happened to you? What did you do?

- Is it easier to make fun of your friend, or to have a private conversation about the issue with them? Why?

- What kinds of things do you think or say to yourself to help you make a good choice in a situation like this?

- What are other situations similar to this where it was really hard to make a good choice (for example, trying to deal with an issue with your friend)?

Shifts in Friendship

Making and keeping friendships takes effort and skill. Relationships change and evolve as children's interests, identities, and needs shift. Thus, the ups and downs in friendships call for refining and expanding social skills to work out the new demands in relationships. Flexibility will play a fundamental role, as a child will need to negotiate and compromise to take into account different opinions and relate to friends with a range of social abilities.

It is common for close friendships to change or end when a child moves away or when one friend decides to expand to different social groups and becomes distant. As children learn the power of their words and actions, hurtful comments or actions can affect trust. It can be difficult to rebuild trust and at times a child needs to decide to take a break from a friendship and seek new positive relationships. Inevitably, children will encounter rejection and disappointment at some point and having an adult accompany them through those low points can help as they cope, bounce back, and try to renew relationships.

Teacher's Guide to Social and Emotional Learning

Teacher Strategies

- Read books and have conversations about friendships.

- Brainstorm with students about what makes a good friend and what factors cause unhealthy relationships.

- Practice problem-solving skills around the theme of friendship. For instance, create a "Dear Abby" blog on friendships. Help kids come up with typical friendship issues of the age group and have them write suggestions on how to approach these difficulties.

- Have a "friendship ups and downs" box in your classroom in which kids can anonymously write problems that arise during the day, and in a class circle time read some of the papers and discuss how these situations could be addressed.

- Occasionally organize recess activities or lunch tables that allow for kids to play with other children to try fostering new connections between kids.

- Raise social concerns with a parent if you notice their child has no friends or is part of a friendship that is not positive at that point, and give resources and ideas as to how the child can develop social skills.

Child Strategies

- Remember friendships have ups and downs and this is normal.

- Friends can disagree. It is OK to not agree on everything with a friend; you can try to hear each other out and, at the end, agree to disagree if you still don't find a common ground.

- Misunderstandings can happen – sometimes you or your friend can feel hurt because of what someone said or did. It is important you talk it out, apologize, and mend your friendship.

- Take a break. Sometimes friends need a bit of space to play with others or even to be alone. If your friend is suddenly acting differently and is not talking to you, you can try and ask him to see if something is wrong. After talking, if he is still distant give him some space because he may need a break. You might sometimes need a break, too; let your friend know you need some alone time or to spend recess with another friend that day.

- Expand your group of friends. Even if you have close friends, sometimes you or your friend might want to play with others, and that is OK. It may be nice for you both to know more people and include them in your games as well.

IS THIS A GOOD FRIENDSHIP?

Sometimes a good friendship might start to feel different and it may no longer feel fair or positive. If the following things happen in your friendship often and you've tried to work it out but nothing changes, then it may be a good idea to find another group of friends:

- Reject you – if your friends talk behind your back or make fun of you.

- Are bossy – if your friend is always telling you what to do and gets angry if you refuse to do it.

- Use put-downs – if your friend calls you names or embarrasses you in front of others.

- Ignores you – if a friend doesn't talk to you or avoids you when you come close or stands up if you sit next to them.

- Spreads rumors – if your friend tells lies or starts rumors about you.

It can be scary to make new friends, but staying in a mean relationship is hurtful, and, with time, you can find a better friend who treats you well.

98

Parent Strategies

- Provide social opportunities. When children are younger, you can organize play dates, and, as children grow and need more independence, you and your child can explore the types of social venues they may enjoy (such as getting involved in sports, organizing class parties, joining school clubs, etc.).

- Get to know your child's friendship style – let your child share with you about the kind of social interactions that feel more comfortable for her. Your child may feel at ease in larger group settings as they move freely between different groups. Alternatively, perhaps your child does better having one or two closer friends.

- Help your child work through difficult emotions and friendship troubles – a wonderful way to help is to just be there and listen. Once they share, if it is helpful you could remind them that there are different sides to every story and perhaps their friend has a different perspective, or suggest they let time pass and then talk to their friend later.

- Let them choose – it can be difficult to see your child establish friendships that you would not usually pick for them. Perhaps they may find the exact contrast of who they are as a way to balance and vicariously learn from each other. Respect these different friendships and have conversations with your child to stay in the loop. Do

Teacher's Guide to Social and Emotional Learning

intervene if you are concerned that this is not a healthy relationship or if you have safety or behavioral worries. In this case, it is important to calmly share your concerns and talk to your child about how he or she may not be able to control others' decisions, but they can control their own decisions. Work with your child to problem-solve how they could respond to different situations.

• Teach them to be kind – share your expectation that your children do not need to be friends with everyone, but do need to be kind and polite to all.

• It is OK to ask for help. Be approachable and tell your kids that it is OK to ask for help when having problems with friends.

100

Discussion Topics

WHAT ARE CHANGES IN FRIENDSHIPS?

Changes in friendships happen as people grow and become interested in new and different things. They can also happen when someone moves away. Friendships have their ups and downs, but it's important to remember that making and keeping friends takes effort. Good friends talk about their ideas, needs, and opinions and they listen when their friends share the same. They are also flexible and willing to compromise in times of conflict.

DO FRIENDSHIPS LAST FOREVER?

Some do, and some don't. Sometimes when you experience new things and develop new interests, your friends will do the same by your side. However, sometimes people find that they are no longer interested in the same things and that they are enjoying spending time with different people. Even if you feel a friendship fading, it is important to continue to treat your old friend with kindness and respect, and to expect them to do the same for you. If a friend begins to treat you poorly, for example putting you down, ignoring you, or spreading rumors, and does not stop when you speak to them about how that makes you feel, then it is definitely time to let the friendship go.

DISCUSSION QUESTIONS

- Have you been friends with someone for a long time? How has your friendship changed over time?

- Can friends disagree? What should they do when they disagree?

- Is it OK to spend time with new people? What can you do if your friend feels sad about the amount of time you are spending with new people?

- What should you do if someone you have been friends with for a long time starts to treat you poorly?

Role Play

Scenario: Gage and Eric have been playing together for a long time. Now Gage is playing with a new friend. Eric walks up and tells him that he can't play with anyone else and that if he does, Eric will never play with him again.

Setting up the Scene: Please review the guidelines in the "How to use this book" section of the introduction.

Guided Questions: After the students have performed the scenario, ask the following questions *(invite both the actors and the rest of the class to answer)*:

DISCUSS FEELINGS:

- What is Gage feeling?

- What is Eric feeling?

103   Teacher's Guide to Social and Emotional Learning

THINKING ABOUT CHOICES:

- What do you think could happen if Gage says he is upset and that he does not want to play with anyone?

- What could Gage gain by stopping playing with his new friend and instead joining Eric in his game?

- How could Gage play with both friends?

- Do you think it could become a habit for Gage to do what others tell him? What could happen if it becomes a habit?

104

MAKING IT PERSONAL:

Help students relate the scenario to their own lives by asking the following:

- Has a situation like this ever happened to you? What did you do?

- Is it easier to try to do what an old friend tells you to do, or find a way to play with all of your friends? Why?

- What kinds of things do you think or say to yourself to help you make good choices and handle changes in friendships?

- What are other situations similar to this where it was really hard to make a good choice (for example, letting go of friends, or including different friends in your game)?

Teacher's Guide to Social and Emotional Learning

106

Talking to an Adult or Teacher

Every child is different in his/her social abilities, but teaching good communication skills is an essential tool whether a child is shy or very social. When a child needs to ask a question in class, express an opinion in a group, or request help on social or other issues, they will be better equipped to handle the task if they have learned communication skills and have had an opportunity to practice, practice, and practice.

Being able to have a conversation with an adult can be a challenge for many children. Both personality and age can play an important factor in a child's comfort when speaking with adults. For example, even a child who is chatty and usually comfortable around adults may feel more intimidated or reluctant to speak to grown-ups during his/her teenage years. This is why it is important to introduce and model more sophisticated skills as children grow and, at the same time, have a balanced expectation of who your child is and where they are in their development.

Teacher Strategies

- Be approachable – create a relationship of trust and open communication with your students.

- Respect and help develop each child's style of communication.

- Remember that some children will have a harder time speaking to adults, so you might need to reach out to them initially and scaffold and model to increase their self-advocacy.

- Create different ways for students to communicate with you; for instance, keeping an interactive journal with you or having lunches to chat.

Child Strategies

- Remember that speaking to an adult can be really helpful, even when it sometimes may feel a bit uncomfortable in the beginning.

- Talk to your parents and other adults about things you do every day, like what you did in sports or your favorite thing of the day. The more you do this, the more comfortable it will feel.

- When talking to adults, ask them questions such as, "How was your weekend?" or "What did you do today?" or "How are you?"

- If you need to talk to your teacher about something, practice with your parents and figure out what words you could use.

- Ask your parents to help you write your first emails to teachers to ask questions.

- Set a goal to raise your hand at least once in class and share your thoughts on what the group is talking about.

Parent Strategies

- Talk to your child using a rich vocabulary and modeling good listening skills.

- Remind your child to use eye contact when speaking. You can look at your child in the eyes by bending or sitting down to become the child's size.

- Include children in conversations with adults from a young age, for instance by having guests in your home and having your child be part of the conversations.

- Use phrases that invite your child to say more about an event or his/her feelings: "Oh," "Tell me more," "No kidding," and "Really."

- Have your child practice requesting food in restaurants, asking questions in a store, etc.

- Teach self-advocacy by role-playing and coaching your child as to what language they could use when asking for help or requesting something from a teacher.

- Model basic courtesy in conversations, like using "Thank you" and appropriate language based on context. For instance, talk about how they need to use different language with teachers and other adults than with peers or at home, both when speaking in person as well as in email and texting.

- Give compliments when your child does a good job in communicating.

Discussion Topics

WHY DO YOU NEED TO TALK TO ADULTS?

Talking to adults is an important communication skill that can be useful when you find yourself in a situation that you are not sure how to handle. Talking with your parents is something you likely do on a regular basis, but knowing how to talk with other adults, like a teacher or a coach, is necessary as well. For example, you will need to speak with an adult if you have a question in class, if you want to share an idea during a sports practice, or if you need help with a social situation.

IS THERE A RIGHT OR WRONG WAY TO SPEAK TO ADULTS?

Talking to adults is very similar to talking with your peers, with the addition of a few manners that show respect. Most of the adults in your life will be eager to help you when you come to them with a question or problem. If you are feeling nervous about speaking with an adult (for example, a teacher), ask your parents to help you practice. If you communicate with your teacher by email, ask a parent or trusted adult to read your email and offer suggestions before you send it.

Teacher's Guide to Social and Emotional Learning

DISCUSSION QUESTIONS

- Share a time when you felt nervous about speaking with an adult.

- What are some situations in which you might need to speak with an adult or teacher?

- In your opinion, what can a teacher do to help you feel comfortable speaking with them?

- Is there an adult in your life that you find easy to talk to? What makes them so approachable?

Role Play

Scenario: Martin is having trouble understanding his math homework, and he has had many wrong answers on his last couple of take-home worksheets.

Setting up the Scene: Please review the guidelines in the "How to use this book" section of the introduction.

Guided Questions: After the students have performed the scenario, ask the following questions *(invite both the actors and the rest of the class to answer)*:

DISCUSS FEELINGS:

- What is Martin feeling?

- What is the teacher feeling?

113   Teacher's Guide to Social and Emotional Learning

THINKING ABOUT CHOICES:

- What do you think could happen if Martin skips his math homework or just guesses, since he isn't getting the right answers anyway?

- What would Martin gain by doing these things and avoiding getting help?

- What could Martin say to explain to his teacher that he may need help?

- Do you think it could become a habit for Martin to avoid talking to his teacher when he does not understand his class work? What could happen if it becomes a habit?

MAKING IT PERSONAL:

Help students relate the scenario to their own lives by asking the following:

- Has a situation like this ever happened to you? What did you do?

- Is it easier to guess at the answers on class work that you are having a hard time with, or to find time to talk to your teacher to get help? Why?

- What kinds of things do you think or say to yourself to help you talk with your teacher?

- What are other situations similar to this where it was really hard to talk to an adult (for example, sharing an issue you are having)?

Teacher's Guide to Social and Emotional Learning

Managing Emotions

Teacher's Guide to Social and Emotional Learning　　　118

Disappointment

Disappointment is a necessary part of human growth. It helps us develop resilience, motivation, and coping skills to go through life. Throughout our entire lives, we encounter disappointments and losses, from realizing there are limitations to what we can do to not getting our needs immediately met. These manageable frustrations are often accompanied by our caregivers' coaching on how to cope with sadness, disillusionment, and other underlying emotions like anger, hurt, and uncertainty. These are necessary "optimal" disappointments, since they help us learn how to change and rebuild our goals, understand what to expect in life, and develop our resilience for future setbacks. It is important that adults let children experience disappointment and uncomfortable feelings, and then guide them in how to bounce back from adversity.

Teacher Strategies

- Prepare children on how to handle disappointment beforehand when possible. For example, if only one student will be able to have a part in the play or have a certain class job, let the class know and brainstorm with them regarding how they can respond if they are not chosen.

- Help kids come up with positive self-talk to calm themselves down, using phrases like, "Oh well, maybe next time."

- Offer opportunities in which kids are challenged and may not get their desired outcome initially but are able to continue to work to achieve their goal, building resilience and perseverance.

Child Strategies

- Experience and share the feeling. Try to figure out what feelings you may be having and then share those with a close adult or friend: "I really wanted _____; I am so disappointed it didn't work out" or "I worked so hard on that project; I feel so angry that I got a bad grade on it."

- Take a 10,000-foot view. Sometimes when you feel disappointed, everything may seem terrible and immense, but talking to a friend or parent can help you see things from a different view, making problems appear smaller and more manageable.

- Find humor – some cultures tell jokes when things are hard, because laughing can frequently bring a feeling that things are less personal. Watch some funny videos, read comics, laugh with a friend, and enjoy the party.

- Is there something you can change? Explore different ideas on how to make the situation better and try one out.

- Re-frame it in your mind – make a list of why this disappointment could actually have a positive side.

Parent Strategies

- Offer perspective – you can ask questions to guide your child to look at things from a different point of view. You can also share a personal story of one of your own disappointments and how you handled it.

- Listen. Make your home a place in which your child can vent and find a constructive way to share his/her emotions.

- Celebrate – acknowledge that your child took a risk and encourage him/her to try again in a different way.

- Have fun. Help your child change their focus by doing something fun like watching a funny movie or going to a favorite place.

- Revisit disappointments. Look back at what happened and how your child worked through it.

- Help your child come up with solutions or ways to handle it, instead of solving it for them.

- Create a network of family and friends around your child who they can talk to and ask for support, aside from you.

122

Discussion Topics

WHAT IS DISAPPOINTMENT?

Disappointment is a feeling of unhappiness that you might experience when a situation does not go the way you had hoped or planned. For example, you might feel disappointed after studying hard for a test but receiving a low grade or if your family's trip to the beach is suddenly canceled. Disappointing situations like this can make you feel many emotions like sadness, anger, or confusion.

WHAT CAN YOU LEARN FROM DISAPPOINTMENT?

Disappointments are a frustrating, but necessary, part of life that helps us learn how to be strong in difficult situations. Disappointments teach us to recognize our strengths and weaknesses, to set goals and change them when necessary, to accept when a situation cannot be changed, to think creatively, and to try again when at first you don't succeed.

Teacher's Guide to Social and Emotional Learning

DISCUSSION QUESTIONS

- Share a time when you felt disappointed.

- What can you do to feel better in a disappointing situation?

- Who can you talk to when you feel disappointed?

- Why can disappointment be a good thing?

- What advice would you give to a friend who is feeling disappointed?

- What is something you have learned from a disappointing situation?

Role Play

Scenario: Natalie said she was going to sit with Diya at lunch, but instead she is sitting with another girl and seems to be ignoring Diya.

Setting up the Scene: Please review the guidelines in the "How to use this book" section of the introduction.

Guided Questions: After the students have performed the scenario, ask the following questions *(invite both the actors and the rest of the class to answer)*:

DISCUSS FEELINGS:

- What is Diya feeling?

- What is Natalie feeling?

THINKING ABOUT CHOICES:

- What do you think could happen if Diya is mad at Natalie and gives her the cold shoulder?

- How could being mad at Natalie benefit Diya?

- What could Diya do to handle her disappointment?

- Do you think that it could become a habit for Diya to be mad at her friends when they don't do what they say they will do? Why?

MAKING IT PERSONAL:

Help students relate the scenario to their own lives by asking the following:

- Has a situation like this ever happened to you? What did you do?

- In a situation like this, would it be easier to be mad at your friend and sit with other kids, or ask your friend privately about what happened? Why?

- What kinds of things do you think or say to yourself to help you make a good choice in a situation like this?

- What are other situations like this where it was really hard to make a good choice (for example, your friend doesn't do what they said they would do and you have to remind them, or you feel let down by a friend)?

Teacher's Guide to Social and Emotional Learning

128

Empathy & Compassion

Since its onset, the theory of Emotional Intelligence (EQ) has shifted our understanding of social-emotional skills and placed importance on developing these aptitudes to be successful, connected, and caring individuals. Empathy has a central role within the EQ precept. As Laura Padilla Walker, assistant professor in the School of Family Life at Brigham Young University, states, "Empathy is one of the foundational moral emotions" (Padilla-Walker, L. M. and Christensen, K. J., 2011).

Empathy refers to the ability to take another person's perspective in order to understand how someone may be feeling by reading body language and social cues. Empathy is a sophisticated emotional ability, as it denotes the possibility to understand the complexity of cause and effect and read behavioral signs, which are characteristic of various emotions. Thus, a child will start at an early age to understand that certain cues such as facial expressions, tone, or behaviors can suggest what someone else is feeling. This understanding leads to being able to predict, based on a context or an event, how someone may respond or feel and thus act accordingly in consideration of ethical choices. Furthermore, as abstract thinking emerges, a child's empathy and moral development continues to mature so that we learn how to recognize right and wrong choices and actions. "(Empathy)… is linked to moral action. It's a feeling that compels people to act compassionately while reasoning alone might not."

Empathy is not only a fundamental aspect of human moral and emotional development, but it is also an important indicator of mental health. If empathy is not developed early on it can lead to uncaring adults and possible psychological disorders. This is why it is crucial that starting at a young age, adults help children recognize their own emotions and develop a caring response to others' feelings and well-being.

Teacher Strategies

- Get children used to identifying, naming, and sharing feelings.

- Introduce a varied feeling vocabulary list to enhance the child's emotional language.

- As situations arise in the school day, ask children to label and discuss their feelings.

- Teach children how to ask each other the right questions so that they feel comfortable sharing their feelings with each other.

- Teach children how to take perspective by putting themselves into the shoes of others.

- Engage in mediation when children are in disagreement and encourage them to consider each other's perspectives and feelings.

Child Strategies

- Read body language. If your friend seems sad, ask if you can help.

- If someone is hurt in the playground, offer to take them to the office.

- Talk to your friends and trusted adults about how you feel.

- Invite your friends to share how they feel and ask them open-ended questions ("why do you feel this way" rather than "do you feel this way" so that they're encouraged to answer beyond just "yes" or "no").

- When you are watching TV or reading a book, think about how the characters must feel (Pizarro and Salovey, 2002).

- If you do not understand what is happening or why people are feeling a certain way, ask them to explain it in a few different ways so that you can try to put yourself in their shoes.

132

Parent Strategies

- Teach empathy by being empathetic in parenting. Don't rush to punishment, but instead focus on hearing the full story.

- Discuss issues that come up at school, always asking how they are feeling and how the other party might be feeling.

- Get your child used to talking about feelings.

- Demonstrate how to talk about feelings by acknowledging and sharing your own feelings with your children when appropriate.

- Discuss how our emotions affect others.

- Demonstrate empathy where needed, whether it's a situation in your own life or in the news.

Discussion Topics

EMPATHY & COMPASSION

WHAT IS EMPATHY?

Empathy is the ability to understand and share another person's feelings. An empathetic person is able to recognize someone else's emotions by paying attention to their facial expressions, body language, and tone of voice. In addition to recognizing emotions, a person with empathy can also share the same feelings.

WHY IS EMPATHY IMPORTANT?

The ability to recognize and share another person's feelings encourages us to treat others with understanding and kindness. Thinking about how someone else might feel in a given situation helps us to make decisions that affect not only ourselves, but everyone involved, in a positive way. In addition, paying attention to other people's feelings is an important part of forming strong and healthy relationships with our friends and family.

WHAT IS COMPASSION AND WHY IS IT IMPORTANT?

Compassion is when we are caring towards others, even if we don't make the same choices they do or if we don't agree with them. Compassion is about feeling for others and treating

Teacher's Guide to Social and Emotional Learning

134

© SmartlyU Inc. All Rights Reserved.

them well. It's important to show compassion to be kind to others, have strong relationships, and ensure that everyone is treated fairly.

DISCUSSION QUESTIONS

- What are some examples of body language that can show how a person is feeling?

- How can you show someone that you care about the way they are feeling?

- What can you say to a friend who appears to be feeling sad or angry?

- Share a time when you used empathy.

- Share a time when someone made you feel better by being empathetic.

- What are the characteristics of a good listener?

Teacher's Guide to Social and Emotional Learning

Role Play

Scenario: Jake notices that David looks really sad today.

Setting up the Scene: Please review the guidelines in the "How to use this book" section of the introduction.

Guided Questions: After the students have performed the scenario, ask the following questions *(invite both the actors and the rest of the class to answer)*:

DISCUSS FEELINGS:

- What is Jake feeling?

- What is David feeling?

THINKING ABOUT CHOICES:

- What do you think could happen if Jake decides play with other friends, since it's not fun to be around David when he is sad?

- What could Jake gain by not finding out what is wrong with David?

- What could Jake do to be a good friend to David?

- Do you think that it could become a habit for Jake to ignore his friends when they're sad? If it became a habit, what could happen?

MAKING IT PERSONAL:

Help students relate the scenario to their own lives by asking the following:

- Has a situation like this ever happened to you? What did you do?

- In a situation like this, would it be easier to ignore your friend or ask them if everything is OK and if they need any help? Why?

- What kinds of things do you think or say to yourself to help you understand what a friend might be feeling in a situation like this?

- What are other situations similar to this where it was really hard to make a good choice (for example, being there for a friend)?

Teacher's Guide to Social and Emotional Learning

Jealousy

From a psychological perspective, jealousy is considered an emotion that is embedded in our evolutionary past as a way to help maintain close relationships (Prinz after Buss and Larsen, 2004). Its function may no longer be as useful in this fashion, since contrary to its purpose, it often hurts relationships and breaks trust rather than safeguarding these connections. Jealousy encompasses the thoughts, feelings, and behaviors that occur when a person believes that a valued relationship is being threatened in some way or when there is a fear of abandonment. Another facet to jealousy boils down to the survival of the sense of self, since it is grounded in insecurity. For instance, a child may feel jealousy when there is a new baby in the family, or if they feel parents are treating a sibling preferentially, or when there is a change in friendships. Jealousy usually involves feelings of anger, insecurity, possessiveness, and competitiveness.

We can help children with feelings of jealousy by teaching them from an early age to recognize emotions with the precept that "feelings are meant to be felt" and are natural.

Teacher's Guide to Social and Emotional Learning

Teacher Strategies

JEALOUSY

- Provide the environment for both parties to air their feelings by acting as a mediator.

- Be neutral and show that you understand both sides by re-stating their story: "I hear you saying…" etc.

- Ask what actions they plan on taking.

- When children act jealously, invite them to share their feelings and used directed questions to help them get to the root issue at hand.

- Provide children with tools for dealing with and managing jealousy (such as deep breathing, remembering their own talents, etc.).

- Praise children for their individual strengths and talents.

Child Strategies

- Remind yourself of your talents and strengths.

- Recognize the strengths of others and their uniqueness.

- Tell yourself you have given your best efforts.

- Breathe deeply and calm yourself.

- Compliment the other person on the thing you are jealous of.

- Think about why you are jealous and how you could let go of it.

- Take yourself out of the situation in which you have jealous feelings, and find another game to play to give yourself time to cool off.

Parent Strategies

- Developing your child's self-esteem and confidence will help them be less likely to feel jealous or insecure.

- Give your child an empathic ear if a situation arises.

- Don't rush to solve the issues, and instead invite your child to think critically by asking questions like, "What are some ways you think you could feel better?"

- Compliment your child when they do the right thing or when they have given their best efforts.

- Let them know that you believe that they will be successful.

- Do not compare your child with other children. This can be the single thing that would most likely instill jealous thoughts.

- Model for your child positive ways to deal with competition and feelings of jealousy.

Discussion Topics

WHAT IS JEALOUSY?

Jealousy is wanting something that someone else has, and it can happen in a variety of situations. For example, you might feel jealous of a friend's relationship with someone else, or you might feel jealous when a family member receives a great present.

HOW CAN JEALOUSY AFFECT YOU?

Jealousy doesn't feel good and it can lead to more bad feelings like sadness, anger, feeling unsure of yourself, and wanting to be better than others. It can also hurt your relationships with others. Often when people feel jealous, they treat those they are jealous of in a mean way. This can have a negative effect on relationships with friends and family.

JEALOUSY

Teacher's Guide to Social and Emotional Learning

JEALOUSY

DISCUSSION QUESTIONS

- Share a time when you felt jealous.

- What are some examples of negative reactions to jealousy?

- What are some examples of positive reactions to jealousy?

- What would be a positive way to deal with feeling jealous of someone's ability to play an instrument?

- What can you say to someone who is feeling jealous of you?

- Is it better to hide jealous feelings or to talk about them? Why?

Role Play

Scenario: Emilia notices that everyone wants to play with the new girl in class.

Setting up the Scene: Please review the guidelines in the "How to use this book" section of the introduction.

Guided Questions: After the students have performed the scenario, ask the following questions *(invite both the actors and the rest of the class to answer)*:

DISCUSS FEELINGS:

- What is Emilia feeling?

- What is the new girl feeling?

Teacher's Guide to Social and Emotional Learning

THINKING ABOUT CHOICES:

- What do you think could happen if Emilia ignores the new student?

- How could Emilia benefit from ignoring the new student?

- What could Emilia do to manage her jealous feelings?

- Do you think that it could become a habit for Emilia to ignore people when she feels insecure and jealous? Why?

MAKING IT PERSONAL:

Help students relate the scenario to their own lives by asking the following:

- Has a situation like this ever happened to you? What did you do?

- In a situation like this, would it be easier to ignore the new student, or to change your attitude and introduce yourself to the new student? Why?

- What kinds of things do you think or say to yourself to help you make a good choice when you feel jealous?

- What are other situations like this where it was really hard to make a good choice (for example, when you are jealous of someone else)?

Loneliness

It is not uncommon for elementary-age children to complain of loneliness and it can be a normal way of coping with changes and relationships. Loneliness could be a result of a variety of reasons, such as:

- Shifts in friendships; for instance, losing a best friend because they have moved or changes in friendship groups.

- Not wanting to play what the rest of the children are playing.

- Being excluded because a child may not have the social skills to connect with peers.

- Feeling different and becoming isolated.

Get to the root of why the child feels lonely. Most often children feel that way on some days and not on others and this may not be cause for concern.

- If allowed by your child's school, observe your child in social situations and get input from their teacher.

- Persistent complaints need an adult intervention.

Teacher Strategies

- Facilitate an introduction to another student who might make a good friend.

- Role-play situations to help children learn how to join a game or introduce themselves.

- Arrange to have a buddy system so the buddy can introduce the student to others.

- Observe for exclusionary behaviors in class and at recess.

- Create opportunities for group work and teams in class activities.

- Teach children friendly behaviors to initiate conversation.

Child Strategies

- Find something in common with one student. Maybe both of you like playing the same games at recess.

- Practice ways to introduce yourself or join a game.

- Use friendly behaviors: smile, introduce yourself, listen to others, and add to discussions.

- Ask an adult to introduce you to children you would like to play with.

- Pair up with different children for group projects in class to meet new people.

- Find games that you can play both by yourself and with other children.

LONELINESS

Parent Strategies

- Arrange play dates at a park or home.

- Observe your child and make note of their interaction; if you see behavior that is not friendly, intervene and offer suggestions.

- Ask what the other kids play at school and introduce that sport to your child.

- Create opportunities to meet new kids in school by enrolling children in after-school activities.

- Follow up with the teacher.

Discussion Topics

WHY DO PEOPLE FEEL LONELY?

Feeling lonely is part of life and can happen for many reasons. It is even possible to feel lonely when there are many people around. People often feel lonely when their relationships with others change. For example, you might feel lonely because your best friend moved away or has been spending time with someone else. You might feel lonely if you have been left out of a group or if you are not interested in the group activity.

WHAT IF THE LONELINESS DOESN'T GO AWAY?

When feelings of loneliness last for a long time, they can make people feel as though they are all by themselves. Sometimes lonely people think they are lonely because they did something wrong, even if they didn't do anything wrong. This is why it is important to take positive action when you are feeling alone; for example, using friendly behaviors like smiling, listening to others, and participating in conversations. Asking the advice of a friend or trusted adult can be helpful as well.

DISCUSSION QUESTIONS

- Share a time when you experienced loneliness.

- What are some examples of positive actions you can take when feeling lonely?

- Other than school, where might you meet new people?

- How can your own interests and hobbies help you connect with other people?

- What advice would you give to a friend who is feeling lonely?

- Who can you talk to when you feel lonely?

154

Role Play

Scenario: Victoria's best friend Kimberly is moving far away because of her dad's new job.

Setting up the Scene: Please review the guidelines in the "How to use this book" section of the introduction.

Guided Questions: After the students have performed the scenario, ask the following questions *(invite both the actors and the rest of the class to answer)*:

DISCUSS FEELINGS:

- What is Victoria feeling?

- What is Kimberly feeling?

LONELINESS

THINKING ABOUT CHOICES:

- What do you think could happen if Victoria is sad a lot, since she might not see her best friend again?

- How would it benefit Victoria to spend her time feeling sad?

- What could Victoria do to feel better?

- Do you think it could become a habit for Victoria to let loneliness take over when she's sad? What could happen if it becomes a habit?

MAKING IT PERSONAL:

Help students relate the scenario to their own lives by asking the following:

- Has a situation like this ever happened to you? What did you do?

- Is it easier to make some new friends, or to just be sad in such a situation? Why?

- What kinds of things do you think or say to yourself to help you make a good choice and make new friends in a situation like this?

- What are other situations similar to this where it was really hard to make a good choice (for example, trying to figure out how to deal with loneliness)?

LONELINESS

Giving Compliments

Compliments have a powerful social and psychological meaning and function. Being able to give and receive compliments is an assertiveness skill that helps build relationships, nurture self-esteem, and enrich conversations. There is an art to giving compliments, and it is a valuable skill that enables people to look beyond oneself, find something that is unique or special about another person, and convey recognition of that special trait in a positive way. Making someone else feel appreciated can bring a sense of gratification for the person giving a compliment. Similarly, receiving compliments helps build a sense of worth and build positive self-image.

Complimenting is a social interaction that can feel awkward and uncomfortable when it does not feel genuine or is done in the wrong context with an untimely tone or wording. Even when the compliment is just right, for some it may still feel difficult to accept this nice gesture.

Learning the skill of giving or receiving a compliment can help a child appreciate his or her social value and practicing or developing this skill further can help to enrich his or her connections with others.

Teacher's Guide to Social and Emotional Learning

Teacher Strategies

- Model how to give compliments and show appreciation when recognizing someone's qualities.

- Dedicate a time (during opening circle in the mornings, after an event, at the end of the year, etc.) when kids give compliments. Start by guiding a conversation as to what makes a compliment a good one (that it is specific, that it is real and sounds genuine, that body language is used when giving a compliment) and do some activities.

- Discuss how it feels to receive a compliment, and, if it feels awkward for some, explore how it could feel good. Have students practice responding to a compliment.

- Class activities can include: in small groups, write notes for each member and have the kids decorate their desks with them; have them write compliments on post-its and give a "pat on the back" as they put the post-it on each other's backs; have students draw their silhouette on a poster board and everyone in the class go around writing compliments for each other; students can write letters of appreciation for each other and read them out loud; create an "appreciation wall" in which kids add comments for each other every day.

Child Strategies

When receiving a compliment:

- A compliment is intended to make you feel good. Show that you are listening to the other person by looking at them and smiling. If you frown or look down or away, the other person may not be sure you like the compliment.

- Say "Thanks!" or "That is very kind."

- Avoid rejecting the compliment by saying things like "No, that's not really true," "You're exaggerating," or "I don't do that well."

When giving a compliment:

- Make it real. Find something that you can say that is true for that person. People can tell the difference between a sincere comment and a fake one. For instance, you can find a quality that you really like and say, "You really are great at basketball," or "You are cool and funny."

- Be specific about the compliment; choosing, "Those shoes are really cool" instead of "You look good today" makes the person feel that you really noticed them.

- Compliments on how people look are great, but it is more powerful to make compliments on how a person acts and behaves. For instance, "You always think of others," or "You tell the best jokes ever."

161 Teacher's Guide to Social and Emotional Learning

Parent Strategies

Model this skill by giving compliments to your child and people around you.

- Guide your child in how to recognize the qualities of others.

- Before your child goes to sleep, have him/her come up with one or two things that he/she appreciates about someone, or something that they appreciated.

- Teach your child to be appropriate and use words that will make the other person feel good and not uncomfortable. For example, comments about someone's body like "You look thin" or "That outfit makes you look taller" can be inappropriate, especially if you do not know that person well.

- Help your child come up with compliments beforehand. Encourage them to think about what they can compliment another person on and the words they will use.

- Demonstrate how to give a simple compliment (don't overdo it; a couple of sentences will do).

162

Discussion Topics

WHAT IS A COMPLIMENT?

To compliment someone means to say something nice to them or about them. It feels great to get a compliment and can feel great to give them as well. You might give someone a compliment when you notice something that makes them unique or special, when you appreciate something they have done for you or someone else, when you admire their skills, or when you are impressed by their accomplishments. When receiving a compliment, it is important to show that you are listening to the other person by looking at them and smiling. Acknowledge the compliment by saying "Thanks" or "That is very kind." Learning to give and receive compliments can help you build relationships and participate positively in conversations.

IS THERE A WRONG WAY TO GIVE A COMPLIMENT?

Compliments are meant to make people feel good and should be given honestly. When giving a compliment, make it real. Find something that you can say that is true for that person. People can tell the difference between a sincere comment and a fake one. When a compliment is given with a negative or sarcastic tone, it can feel awkward or uncomfortable. The compliment may be mistaken for teasing. It is also important to choose compliments that are appropriate. For example, commenting on someone's physical appearance can make them feel uncomfortable, particularly if you do not know them well. Instead, look for ways to compliment the positive qualities that you notice about their personality and abilities.

DISCUSSION QUESTIONS

- What is the best compliment you have ever received?

- What can you say when you receive a compliment?

- Share a time when you received a compliment that did not feel sincere.

- What makes a "good" compliment?

- What makes a "bad" compliment?

- Why is it important to include compliments in your conversations with others?

Role Play

Scenario: Emma tells Isaac that she is not sure whether to play soccer or lacrosse this summer. Isaac knows that Emma is good at both.

Setting up the Scene: Please review the guidelines in the "How to use this book" section of the introduction.

Guided Questions: After the students have performed the scenario, ask the following questions *(invite both the actors and the rest of the class to answer)*:

DISCUSS FEELINGS:

- What is Isaac feeling?

- What is Emma feeling?

THINKING ABOUT CHOICES:

- What do you think could happen if Isaac changes the subject because he is not sure what to say to Emma?

- How would changing the subject benefit Isaac?

- What could Isaac say to Emma to be friendly and supportive?

- Do you think that it could become a habit for Isaac to avoid giving compliments because he does not know what to say? What could happen if it becomes a habit?

- What could happen if Isaac just says, "I don't know; whatever" to Emma?

MAKING IT PERSONAL:

Help students relate the scenario to their own lives by asking the following:

- Has a situation like this ever happened to you? What did you do?

- In a situation like this, would it be easier to change the subject or to tell your friend that it's a hard choice because she's good at both sports? Why?

- What kinds of things do you think or say to yourself to help you compliment a friend in a situation like this?

- What are other situations like this where it was really hard to make a good choice (for example, if someone else does a good job, or if you are trying to compliment someone)?

Teacher's Guide to Social and Emotional Learning

Identifying Triggers/ Techniques to Calm Down

Triggers are cues that bring forth sudden feelings or memories. A trigger can be something that someone says or does, or a specific situation that prompts an array of strong emotions which can include anger, stress, sadness, happiness, etc. Some common examples of triggers specific to children could be when a peer doesn't follow the rules in a game, when someone makes a comment about the child's family, or abilities, or when he or she is hungry or tired. Triggers are very personal, and this is why it is a good idea to help a child recognize what sets them off so that they can find ways to regulate the emotions that arise.

The ability to regulate emotions is crucial. In this process, the child learns skills of flexibility, adaptability, and tolerance to frustration as they begin to identify their personal warning signs and figure out ways to cope with their feelings. Feelings are meant to be felt, yet the child has to learn how to express emotions in constructive ways and be able to calm down.

Teacher's Guide to Social and Emotional Learning

Teacher Strategies

- Help the child recognize and name their triggers by asking what happened before they got angry or upset; help them read the situation prior to the feeling.

- Hand out a drawing of a silhouette of a body and have the children color in where they feel anger, sadness, and happiness, and how they recognize this in their own bodies (their heart beats faster, their hands get sweaty, etc.).

- Children can create "Calming Strips" which are pieces of paper on which they write or draw three things that they can do in school when they are upset.

  - Have weighted vests or heavy stuffed animals that kids can hold which will help "ground" them and calm them down.

  - Have a calming place within the classroom that is safe and private; it could be the "chill seat" or the "take a break corner" with pillows, stuffed animals, and squishy balls.

  - Teach the children to use "I" statements: "I feel… when you… because… I want…"

  - Have a signal or code to indicate that the child needs to use a strategy that was discussed previously.

  - Instill transition times and a visual schedule (what is coming next) for children who have a difficult time with changes.

Child Strategies

- Pay attention to your body. Where do you feel anger, sadness, nervousness?

- If you had a feeling thermometer, how could you tell when your feeling is going to go up really high? Can you notice it before it reaches a high level?

- Think of three things you can do when you feel upset. Some strategies are:

  - Take a break and walk away from the situation. Once you are calmer you can come back.

  - Go and drink some water.

  - Breathe in through your nose and out through your mouth, counting to eight.

  - Listen to calming music.

  - Do finger painting or drawing.

  - Play with outdoors.

  - Rest or eat something.

Parent Strategies

- Model appropriate reaction to emotions by keeping calm and not overreacting. State that you are feeling angry or frustrated and explain how you are going to calm down.

- Help your child calm down by using your body language and speaking to them on their same level, making eye contact, and using gentle gestures and tone of voice.

- Help your child label his/her feelings and express them with words.

- Help them figure out some productive outlets of emotions. Some ideas include using imagery, meditation, humor, art …

- Help them change their perspective by teaching them to take someone else's view, see the big picture, accurately interpret a situation, and delay gratification.

Discussion Topics

WHAT IS A TRIGGER?

Everyone feels emotions like sadness, anger, and anxiety from time to time. Sometimes, these feelings are caused by a trigger. A "trigger" is a signal that causes us to experience sudden feelings or memories. This could be something that someone says or does, a situation that reminds you of another time, or even a physical sensation, like the feel of a piece of clothing or a smell.

WHY DO YOU NEED TO KNOW YOUR TRIGGERS?

Triggers are very personal and different for each individual. It is important to recognize the triggers in your life and to find ways to calm down when you experience strong emotions. Learning to be flexible, adapting to uncomfortable situations, and managing frustration are part of growing up. Feelings are meant to be felt and learning to express them in an appropriate way allows us to solve problems and communicate effectively.

Teacher's Guide to Social and Emotional Learning

DISCUSSION QUESTIONS

- What are some triggers in your life?

- What are some ways to calm down when you feel strong emotions?

- Hunger is a common trigger among children. What is the difference between the way a two-year-old and a twelve-year-old might express hunger?

- What are common triggers for very young children?

- What are common triggers for older children and adults?

- Is it important to recognize other people's triggers? Why?

Role Play

Scenario: Jamie overheard his friend Brooke saying that he was stupid.

Setting up the Scene: Please review the guidelines in the "How to use this book" section of the introduction.

Guided Questions: After the students have performed the scenario, ask the following questions *(invite both the actors and the rest of the class to answer)*:

DISCUSS FEELINGS:

- What is Jamie feeling?

- What is Brooke feeling?

Teacher's Guide to Social and Emotional Learning

THINKING ABOUT CHOICES:

- What do you think could happen if Jamie walks up to Brooke and tells her she is stupid?

- How would Jamie benefit by talking to his friend when he's still hurt and upset?

- What are some ways that Jamie could calm down before talking to his friend?

- Do you think that it could become a habit for Jamie to talk to his friends about his feelings before he has calmed down? Why?

- What could happen if Jamie decides never to talk to Brooke again?

MAKING IT PERSONAL:

Help students relate the scenario to their own lives by asking the following:

- Has a situation like this ever happened to you? What did you do?

- In a situation like this, would it be easier to talk to your friend while you are still angry, or to wait until you're feeling calm to tell them how you feel? Why?

- What kinds of things do you think or say to yourself to help you realize that you are too upset to talk to your friend, and to calm yourself down in a situation like this?

- What are other situations like this where it was really hard to make a good choice (for example, if you're upset with your friend and want to talk to them about it right away, or if you're having a hard time calming down)?

IDENTIFYINGTRIGGERS/TECHNIQUESTOCALMDOWN

178

Personal Development

179

Apologizing

Being able to give and to receive an apology are both complex social skills. It is a profound interaction that entails empathy, responsibility, humbleness, and the ability to forgive, amongst other competencies. Giving an apology means that the child is able to take responsibility, especially when they have hurt someone. It is an opportunity to learn about remorse and offering reparation, and shows that children are learning how to understand conflict and reconciliation as well as how to manage themselves and their relationships. In teaching children to genuinely apologize, we are helping them develop their understanding of the thoughts and feelings of others and how to take care of their relationships.

It is also a learning opportunity for the child who is receiving the apology. While forgiving can be difficult, it offers an opportunity to let go of anger, embarrassment, guilt, and hurt. For both children it is an experience that strengthens connection as they resolve and build relationships.

Teacher Strategies

- Coach students on how to give a genuine apology.

- Provide language for receiving an apology.

- Model different ways in which kids can offer and accept apologies, including "I" statements.

- Brainstorm ways to "fix" or "mend" different scenarios, including, for instance, how to build trust again, how to make someone feel better, etc.

- It is not helpful to force someone to give an apology, but teachers can help coach both children to problem-solve and use some conflict resolution skills to mend a situation.

- Provide a "feeling vocabulary" so that the children can increase their empathy and have further tools as they learn how to cope with conflict.

182

Child Strategies

Giving an apology

- Take time to cool off before trying to fix the problem, so that the other person is able to hear you and you are able to say things calmly.

- Recognize and own up to what you did (and remember that even if you do, the other person might still not be ready to trust or forgive you).

- Use phrases like, "I am sorry. I didn't mean to hurt you," "Is there something I can do to help?" or "Sorry, that was my fault."

Receiving an apology

- Listen to the other person's apology.

- Share your feelings and what would make you feel better. For example, "I felt hurt when you did that" or, "It would be helpful if you help me put it together again."

- Remember you still may feel hurt and building trust will take time.

- Use phrases like, "Thank you for apologizing," "We can still be friends," "I accept your apology," or, "I forgive you."

Parent Strategies

- Help children take time to cool off. You can acknowledge that feelings were hurt or that there was a mistake and that it will be important to figure out how to address this later.

- Coach your child by asking questions like, "How do you think the other person is feeling?" or "Can you think of anything you could say or do to help fix the situation?" or "What are words you could use to apologize or to accept an apology?"

- Recognize and validate hurt feelings on both ends.

- Praise your child for the courage and integrity it takes to either apologize or forgive.

Discussion Topics

WHAT IS APOLOGIZING?

Apologizing, or giving an apology, is the act of accepting responsibility and saying you're sorry when you have done something that is against the rules or has hurt someone else. Being able to apologize shows that you care about the thoughts and feelings of others and that you want to take care of your relationships.

WHY IS IT IMPORTANT TO ACCEPT APOLOGIES?

Knowing how to accept an apology is just as important as knowing how to give one. Forgiving someone after they have hurt you shows that you care about the relationship and are willing to let go of the anger, embarrassment, or hurt that has come between you. The ability to overcome painful situations is one of the characteristics of a strong relationship.

DISCUSSION QUESTIONS

- Share a time when you apologized for something.

- What is the hardest part of apologizing?

- What are some words and phrases that you can use when apologizing?

- Share a time when you accepted an apology.

- What is the hardest part of accepting an apology?

- Should you always accept an apology right away? Why or why not?

Role Play

Scenario: The class is lining up and Zane accidentally shoves Joel, who is standing in front of him. This causes the other children in the line to fall down.

Setting up the Scene: Please review the guidelines in the "How to use this book" section of the introduction.

Guided Questions: After the students have performed the scenario, ask the following questions *(invite both the actors and the rest of the class to answer)*:

DISCUSS FEELINGS:

- What is Zane feeling?

- What are Joel and the other children feeling?

Teacher's Guide to Social and Emotional Learning

THINKING ABOUT CHOICES:

- What do you think could happen if Zane does not apologize?

- What would Zane gain by not doing anything about the situation?

- How could Zane apologize to Joel and the other children?

- Do you think it could become a habit for Zane to not apologize when he does things by accident? What could happen if it became a habit?

MAKING IT PERSONAL:

Help students relate the scenario to their own lives by asking the following:

- Has a situation like this ever happened to you? What did you do?

- Is it easier to apologize and explain what happened, or not do anything? Why?

- What kinds of things do you think or say to yourself to help you apologize in a situation like this?

- What are other situations similar to this where it was really hard to make a good choice (for example, apologizing for something that you don't feel was your fault)?

Teacher's Guide to Social and Emotional Learning

Coping with Peer Pressure

Parents, mentors, and teachers will often guide children through difficult decisions and help them sort through feelings and possible options to make sound choices. However, when the adult is not present, children will be faced with making decisions, and balancing external demands such as peer pressure with their own developing moral code.

Children learn from children. In fact, much of a child's learning about social rules and behavior comes from observation and imitation of peers ("Psychological Modelling," Bandura A., 1971). Thus, peer pressure can be a powerful force, for both constructive and detrimental outcomes. In particular, resisting negative peer pressure can be really hard, as children may be afraid of being rejected by their peer group. Teaching children how to recognize peer pressure and how to handle it is an essential skill that will be helpful when welcoming positive peer pressure such as participating in a school club with friends or getting good grades, and tackling risky decisions such as cheating, stealing, and later on alcohol or drug use.

Teacher Strategies

- Talk about it. Have students define what peer pressure is, and discuss the difference between both spoken and unspoken peer pressure, and positive and negative peer pressure.

- Role play – create scenarios and have students role play ways to respond to a variety of situations. Help students practice assertiveness and refusal skills individually and in small groups.

- Ask students to write and share about times they felt peer pressure and how they dealt with it.

- Have students practice reading body language and reflect on how they can tell when someone is feeling uncomfortable or does not want to do something.

- Create spaces for parent conversations. Work closely with the school counselor to provide parent workshops or discussions in which parents can talk and compare notes about different strategies and similar situations that they encounter at home.

Child Strategies

- Listen to your "gut." If you know that what is going on makes you feel uncomfortable, it probably is not a good idea and it is negative peer pressure.

- Name the problem: "but... that's cheating" or, "You're asking me to _____ (lie, steal, be mean...)."

- Say, "No" in a clear and strong way. You can also say, "No, that's not cool" or, "Nope, I really don't want to" or, "That's not really a good idea," or even put it on your parents, saying, "My parents would ground me forever."

- Avoid the situation – if you see a group is talking about something that you do not like, walk away and find someone else to talk to.

- Suggest something else to do – "Why don't we go and shoot some baskets?"

- Stand up for others. If you see someone is being a victim of negative peer pressure, help them by saying, "Hey, it sounds like he really doesn't want to do it" or, "I'm with you, let's do something different."

- Find an ally – standing up to peer pressure can be easier when you're not alone. Choose a friend who will back you up so that both of you can avoid the pressure together.

Parent Strategies

- Validate your child's opinions – ask your child about his thoughts on different topics and give him opportunities to make choices.

- Practice come-backs. Talk and role-play different scenarios she could encounter and what she could say, like, "No, I really don't want to," "My parents would be mad at me if I do that," or "Let's go ride our bikes instead."

- Help your child think about consequences. When a parent asks, "What were you thinking?" the answer is often, "I don't know, I wasn't thinking." Ask him to draw or write what he imagines could be consequences to different scenarios so he can practice this skill ahead of time.

- To help kids get out of uncomfortable or unsafe situations, come up with a code like, "Is grandma there yet?", which means you should come get them, no questions asked.

- Get to know your child's friends. Organize play dates and constructive activities for your kids to make positive connections and for you to see who they are close to.

- Talk to other parents. Listening and sharing is a wonderful way to realize that not everyone has that game your child wants or has the privileges your child is demanding, and also to find out how other parents cope with similar situations.

Discussion Topics

WHAT IS PEER PRESSURE?

Peer pressure is when someone from your peer group, like a friend or classmate, influences your decision to either do or not do something. People give in to peer pressure for many reasons. They might be afraid of being rejected by their friends, they may not want to be seen as different from the group, or they may not know how to get themselves out of the situation. When dealing with peer pressure it is important to have confidence in your own decisions. Listen to your "gut." If someone is telling you to do something that makes you feel uncomfortable, it probably is not a good idea.

IS PEER PRESSURE ALWAYS BAD?

While the term "peer pressure" is usually thought of as negative, your friends and classmates can put positive pressure on you as well. For example, your friends might encourage you to join an after-school activity or club. Similarly, you might feel pressure to study hard and complete your homework knowing your friends regularly get good grades.

Teacher's Guide to Social and Emotional Learning

DISCUSSION QUESTIONS

- Share a time when you experienced peer pressure.

- Share a time when you stood up to peer pressure. What did you say?

- Share a time when you felt pressure from friends to participate in something positive.

- What can you do or say if you see your friends peer pressuring someone else?

- What are some ways to get out of a peer pressure situation?

Role Play

Scenario: All of Ben's friends have the latest video game and talk about it at recess. Ben does not have the video game, and he feels very left out.

Setting up the Scene: Please review the guidelines in the "How to use this book" section of the introduction.

Guided Questions: After the students have performed the scenario, ask the following questions *(invite both the actors and the rest of the class to answer)*:

DISCUSS FEELINGS:

- What is Ben feeling?

- What are Ben's friends feeling?

Teacher's Guide to Social and Emotional Learning

THINKING ABOUT CHOICES:

- What do you think could happen if Ben lies and pretends he has the game, too?

- What would Ben gain by lying?

- What could Ben do to handle the peer pressure he's feeling?

- Do you think that lying could become a habit for Ben? Why? What could happen if it became a habit?

198

MAKING IT PERSONAL:

Help students relate the scenario to their own lives by asking the following:

- Has a situation like this ever happened to you? What did you do?

- Would it be easier to be honest or to pretend to have the game in a situation like this? Why?

- What kinds of things do you think or say to yourself to help you not feel the peer pressure in a situation like this?

- What are other situations like this where it was really hard to make a good choice (for example, feeling left out from your friends, or wanting to pretend something so that you can fit in)?

COPING WITH PEER PRESSURE

Teacher's Guide to Social and Emotional Learning

Dealing with Competition

Competition can be considered a path of growth, opportunity, and self-evaluation by comparing ourselves to others. However, how we view competition also has cultural components and plays out differently based on our personalities and views of ourselves and of others.

Healthy competition can help a child develop grit, resilience, compassion, motivation, and discipline ("How Children Succeed: Grit, Curiosity, and the Hidden Power of Character," Paul Tough, 2012). It can also be a positive experience if it is taught in a way in which working with others, problem-solving, enjoyment, and personal best are valued. Learning how to deal with competition also helps children develop mechanisms to cope with losing and winning. Sports, games, projects, and tournaments are opportunities for children to develop empathy, learn how to treat others, work hard, respect adults, follow written and unwritten rules, be honest, and be good losers and winners. In this way, competition can help children develop self-worth and become comfortable with who they are.

Teacher Strategies

- Let all your students know that you believe that they will be successful.

- Ask for their best effort.

- Stress learning over winning.

- Value process over final product.

- Teach healthy competition through competitive games and activities.

- Share stories such as sports news of how teams compete and what they learn from the game.

202

Child Strategies

- Do your best.

- Compliment others who are better than you at something. Remember everyone has areas of strengths and challenges.

- Understand that being the best at everything isn't the most important part, and that it's better to enjoy yourself and have a good time.

- If you make a mistake, think about what you learned from it. There are always more things to learn, and if you don't win, that's OK.

- Talk with your parents or teacher about how you can create goals for yourself.

Teacher's Guide to Social and Emotional Learning

Parent Strategies

- Let your child know when they have given their best efforts and when you're proud of them.

- Share stories of famous people who have won and lost.

- Provide opportunities to play games of chance such as old maid, bingo, chess, etc.

- Get children involved in games in which children get practice in learning how to cope with feelings of losing and winning.

- For younger children, set up small competitive games like, "How many hoops can you get in five minutes?"

- Follow rules and don't bend the rules to get a winner.

- Let them know that you believe that they will be successful.

- Do not compare your child with other children. This can be the single most influential factor that will instill a sense of unhealthy competition in your child.

- Stress learning over winning.

- Set realistic goals for games and activities.

- Value and compliment the process and effort over the final product (winning games, grades, etc.).

Discussion Topics

WHAT IS COMPETITION?

Competition is the act of trying to be as good as or better than others at a given task or skill, often with the goal to win. Competition is a part of everyday life. For example, we compete to win when we play sports. Some people have competitive personalities and look for ways to make every situation into a competition, like trying to get the best grades, be the first in line, or be the loudest person in the room. Winning feels great, but unfortunately, it is not possible to win every time you compete. Worrying too much about winning can get in the way of enjoying an experience and can cause you to lose focus. It is important to remember that trying your best and having fun is just as important as winning.

WHAT IS A SORE LOSER?

It is no fun to play with someone who becomes angry or sad when they do not win. A person who acts this way would be considered a sore loser. It is important to be a graceful loser. Even if you are not the winner, take comfort in the fact that you tried your hardest, had fun, and maybe even learned something. Take time to compliment the winner with kind words like, "Good job!"

DISCUSSION QUESTIONS

- Is it more important to win or have a good time?

- Share a time when you won a competition.

- Share a time when you lost a competition but still had fun.

- Do you like to play games with people who only care about winning? Why or why not?

- What advice would you give to a friend who is feeling sad after losing a competition?

206

Role Play

Scenario: Nathan is really excited because he got 100% on his spelling test, but then he notices than his friend Isaac got a low score. Isaac wants to know how Nathan did, but Nathan doesn't want him to feel bad.

Setting up the Scene: Please review the guidelines in the "How to use this book" section of the introduction.

Guided Questions: After the students have performed the scenario, ask the following questions *(invite both the actors and the rest of the class to answer)*:

DISCUSS FEELINGS:

- What is Nathan feeling?

- What is Isaac feeling?

Teacher's Guide to Social and Emotional Learning

THINKING ABOUT CHOICES:

- What do you think could happen if Nathan lies about his score and says he did poorly, too?

- What would Nathan gain by lying?

- What could Nathan say to Isaac to be honest and not make him feel bad?

- Do you think that it could become a habit for Nathan to pretend he has a different score than he really does? What could happen if it became a habit?

DEALING WITH COMPETITION

MAKING IT PERSONAL:

Help students relate the scenario to their own lives by asking the following:

- Has a situation like this ever happened to you? What did you do?

- In a situation like this, would it be easier to lie about how well you did or offer to help your friend study for the next test? Why?

- What kinds of things do you think or say to yourself to help you make a good choice in a situation like this?

- What are other situations similar to this where it was really hard to make a good choice (for example, balancing being proud of how well you did with not making your friend feel bad)?

Effective Communication

Communication is an essential instrument that enables us to convey our thoughts, emotions, needs, expectations, and hopes. We give meaning, shape, and transform our world through language.

Some people are inherently quieter communicators who prefer to keep things to themselves, while others are more open about their thoughts, feelings, and ideas. How we communicate takes shape through daily interactions with family, peers, and the culture and environment around us, so that what is said (and not said) and how it is communicated passes through a personal and social filter. There are many ways to communicate, and effective communication is best taught when it enhances the child's personality, character traits, and personal strengths.

Teaching children communication skills is a way in which we provide tools so that they can effectively deliver and receive messages. This learning process should respectfully build on the individual's communication style, strengths, and challenges.

Teacher Strategies

- Remember that each child communicates differently and has a different communication comfort zone. Teachers should be respectful of individual styles, strengths, and challenges, while still helping build effective communication skills. For example, if a child is having a particularly difficult time speaking in public, teachers can help the child feel more comfortable by suggesting the child present to just one or two trusted people, and then present to a larger group, and so on. Figuring out what each child needs to be a more effective communicator is key here.

- Provide public speaking opportunities. No matter the age, children benefit from practicing speaking in front of others, such as with show and tell or project presentations.

- Model and build good communication skills in class – provide language to help children formulate their thoughts. For instance, introducing and practicing "I" statements can be a powerful building block for fomenting future communication abilities.

- Guide a child to reflect and organize their thoughts and feelings by using phrases like "so you feel…" or "it sounds like you…" or "you would like to know if…."

- Play games that introduce and have fun with the theme of communication, like playing telephone or doing improv.

Child Strategies

- Make eye contact and smile when speaking to others – this helps establish a good first interaction. It is important to keep in mind that people from other cultures might communicate using body language differently. For instance, in some cultures, avoiding eye contact is a way of showing respect.

- Be clear as you speak – for instance, if you are doing a presentation in front of your class, practice your speech beforehand and pay attention to your pronunciation so that you do not rush while you are talking. You can make note cards with the main points to keep you on track.

- Take turns and don't interrupt – this way you show your respect to the person you are talking to.

- Show you are listening. You can show others you are paying attention by nodding your head or repeating something they just said.

- Enter a conversation respectfully. Approach a group quietly, smile to the people having the conversation, listen to what they are saying, and find a good time, such as when there is a pause in the conversation, to share your thoughts on the topic.

- End a conversation on a good note. You can say something like, "It was nice talking to you."

Parent Strategies

- Have conversations. Through daily chats on a variety of topics, you can model both speaking as well as listening skills. For instance, you can nod your head or say things like, "That is a great observation" or "What else?" to show that you are listening. Show your interest in what they have to say and expect that they listen to you as well.

- Share stories. Storytelling is a wonderful way to bring imagination, language, and meaning to conversations. Have your child tell stories and organize her thoughts to share a story in a way that is clear. This way she can also learn to change her wording or message if she is not understood.

- Teach your child to actively listen. Guide your child in practicing skills such as waiting silently and listening to the other person without interrupting, repeating or summarizing what he heard in a conversation, and giving an appropriate response to a comment.

- Change some unhelpful habits – point out things that they could work on to become better communicators such as avoiding interrupting, rambling, or changing topic abruptly.

- Access opportunities to practice – explore in conjunction with your child if he may benefit from and enjoy being in theater, a debate club, or a public speaking class to enhance his confidence and communication abilities.

Discussion Topics

WHAT IS EFFECTIVE COMMUNICATION?

Communication is the process of sharing thoughts, feelings, and ideas with others. People communicate in a variety of ways including through speech, writing, and body language. In addition to helping us meet our basic needs, communication allows us to build personal relationships, as well as relationships between communities and cultures.

WHAT DOES EFFECTIVE COMMUNICATION LOOK AND SOUND LIKE?

Effective communication happens when thoughts, feelings, and ideas are shared in such a way that they can be heard and understood. For example, when communicating through speech, it is important for the speaker to use a loud clear voice and to speak at an appropriate speed in order to be understood. A speaker can also vary their tone and pitch in order to create interest. A confident posture and eye contact also serve to engage an audience.

Teacher's Guide to Social and Emotional Learning

EFFECTIVE COMMUNICATION

DISCUSSION QUESTIONS

- What types of communication do you use in your everyday life?

- Share a time when you spoke in front of a group of people. Was it easy or difficult? Why?

- What are the characteristics of a strong speaking voice?

- What are some examples of engaging body language?

- Do you think social media tools, like email or Snapchat, are an effective form of communication? Why or why not?

- What is meant by the phrase, "It's not what you say; it's how you say it?"

Role Play

Scenario: Mason's friends get really rough when there is a disagreement.

Setting up the Scene: Please review the guidelines in the "How to use this book" section of the introduction.

Guided Questions: After the students have performed the scenario, ask the following questions *(invite both the actors and the rest of the class to answer)*:

DISCUSS FEELINGS:

- What is Mason feeling?

- What are his friends feeling?

THINKING ABOUT CHOICES:

- What do you think could happen if Mason doesn't tell his friends that they should talk it over instead of roughing it out?

- What could Mason gain by not speaking up?

- What could Mason do to show good communication skills?

- Do you think that it could become a habit for Mason to not speak up when he sees his friends roughing it out? What could happen if it becomes a habit?

MAKING IT PERSONAL:

Help students relate the scenario to their own lives by asking the following:

- Has a situation like this ever happened to you? What did you do?

- In a situation like this, would it be easier to ignore the situation or to never play with or talk to your friends? Why?

- What kinds of things do you think or say to yourself to help you speak up in a situation like this?

- What are other situations like this where it was really hard to make a good choice (for example, figuring out how to talk to other kids about how you feel)?

EFFECTIVE COMMUNICATION

220

Honesty, Integrity & Commitment

Honesty, integrity, and commitment are all values that are best learned when adults act as role models by demonstrating and honoring these skills in their own lives.

Honesty means being truthful, knowing what is right, and admitting to mistakes your actions may have caused. Teach children that a wrong, however small, is always a wrong and explain the consequences. When mistakes are made, share actions to correct them.

Integrity is one of the most important values and skills that a child can learn. Although a complex and profound concept – which may seem sometimes abstract and intangible (especially for kids) – we recognize its crucial value in individuals and our society. Integrity speaks to an individual's ability to stay true to their inner core values and beliefs. It has an all-encompassing meaning, which comprises honesty, taking personal responsibility, patience, accountability, and following a moral code. Perhaps a simple way to teach it to children is to let them know that people with integrity "say and do what they mean and mean what they say and do."

Commitment is tightly integrated with integrity. It means that there is follow-through on a given word or activity. For example, when children sign up for a sport, they need to know that their team and coach depend on them. Quitting when things get tough shows a lack of commitment. Talk to children about the benefits of following through, both in the short-term and in the long-term, to help them become dependable individuals.

222

Teacher Strategies

- Explain that by being honest, others build trust in what you say and do.

- Mistakes happen and it is important that children learn the importance of admitting to mistakes.

- Introduce the word integrity and ask the children to try to define it. Share a child-friendly definition, such as "doing something right, because you know this is the right thing to do, even if someone is not watching you."

- Read stories and analyze characters, discussing if they showed integrity in their decisions, actions, and words.

- Compliment students when they act with integrity.

- Talk to the class about examples they see every day in their life and in TV programs, and how this shows integrity or a lack of this quality.

- Explain that commitment means following through with what you said you would do.

- Ask children to share areas in their life where commitment is important, such as showing up when you are playing a team sport, working hard to master a subject, etc.

HONESTY, INTEGRITY & COMMITMENT

Child Strategies

- Define your values – what you think is right or wrong.

- Make sure your actions and words follow what you believe in.

- Do the right thing, even when someone is not watching.

- Be honest and responsible in the day-to-day things. For instance, do not copy homework or turn in work that is not yours, keep your promises, treat others with respect, and admit your mistakes.

- Remember that "honesty" means telling the truth. This means no lying, cheating, or stealing.

- Illustrate or create art projects that show the qualities of honesty, integrity, and commitment.

- Commit to things that you promised to do.

Parent Strategies

- Model integrity in your actions, words, and thoughts. Children will learn to shape their character traits through observing, and are good at picking up underlying messages in what we say or how we act. Thus, pay attention as to how you speak to and about people, be it your child's teacher to someone serving in a restaurant. Make ethical decisions at work and in your day-to-day life.

- Keep your promises and, if you are not able to, talk to your child about the reason behind it.

- Instill your family values by helping your child weave compassion, empathy, and concern for others into their daily life. For instance, speak to them about conflicts that may arise in recess or in their classroom and help guide them to follow these values.

- Help your child take responsibility for their actions and offer an apology when needed.

- Reflect on what mixed messages you may sometimes send and think of how to be more congruent. Talk to your kids about how this process was for you.

Discussion Topics

WHAT IS HONESTY?

The definition of "honesty" is speaking the truth. This means no lying, cheating, or stealing.

WHAT IS INTEGRITY?

Integrity is a person's ability to stay true to who they are and what they believe. Acting with integrity means behaving honestly, taking responsibility for your actions, being patient, and knowing and choosing right from wrong. People with integrity say and do what they mean and mean what they say and do.

WHY ACT WITH INTEGRITY?

Acting with integrity shows others that you can be trusted. People value honesty and respect someone who takes responsibility for their actions. These are the qualities that are highly valued in friendships.

WHAT IS COMMITMENT?

Commitment means following through on what you said you would do. For example if you have committed to a sport, you don't quit when things get tough.

DISCUSSION QUESTIONS

- What values are important to you?

- Why is it important to do the right thing, even if no one is watching?

- Why is it important to admit when you have made a mistake?

- Share some examples of how you use integrity in your life.

- Identify someone who you feel acts with integrity. What is the one thing you admire most about this person?

- Why is it important to keep your promises?

- How does integrity help to build strong friendships?

HONESTY, INTEGRITY & COMMITMENT

Teacher's Guide to Social and Emotional Learning

Role Play

Scenario: Lucia has been doing poorly at math and her parents have signed her up for tutoring. Lucia does not enjoy tutoring.

Setting up the Scene: Please review the guidelines in the "How to use this book" section of the introduction.

Guided Questions: After the students have performed the scenario, ask the following questions *(invite both the actors and the rest of the class to answer)*:

DISCUSS FEELINGS:

- What is Lucia feeling?

- What are Lucia's parents feeling?

THINKING ABOUT CHOICES:

- What do you think could happen if Lucia goes to the tutor but does not try at all?

- What would Lucia gain by not trying?

- What could Lucia say to herself to enjoy tutoring?

- Do you think that it could become a habit for Lucia to not be committed to things that she has to do? What could happen if it became a habit?

MAKING IT PERSONAL:

Help students relate the scenario to their own lives by asking the following:

- Has a situation like this ever happened to you? What did you do?

- In a situation like this, would it be easier to not try or to think of the ways tutoring can help and make the most of it? Why?

- What kinds of things do you think or say to yourself to help you commit to something in a situation like this?

- What are other situations like this where it was really hard to make a good choice (for example, dealing with something you don't like to do, or needing to stick with a commitment)?

Responsibility

Being responsible is a life skill that will benefit a child in school and at home, and is definitely one that will prove valuable as she/he grows into a competent adult. Responsibility is a process, a mindset, and an outlook on one's ability to make decisions and follow through, contributing to a classroom, family, and society. It is taught and developed, yet also takes shape distinctly for each child as it is stems from their character and set of abilities.

As a child starts to take small responsibilities, he/she builds confidence and independence. This is why it is crucial to start from a young age and scaffold this process by providing opportunities to accomplish age-appropriate chores and goals. It is also key to know each child's strengths and areas of challenge to create ways in which he/she can be successful in the process. Remember there are different ways to teach responsibility, from taking care of their clothes and belongings, doing their chores, being accountable in their schoolwork, or being responsible for keeping an eye on their siblings.

Teacher Strategies

- Talk to the children about how many of the classroom routines help promote responsibility, such as having assigned roles (door-holder, teacher's helper, paper-passer, etc.).

- Provide organizers, charts, and opportunities to review routines in order to help children be more independent in their work and in meeting their own needs. For instance, knowing where to find the class materials and taking care of them will help foster a sense of responsibility.

- Invite children to do a personal reflection on their own progress in this area through journaling or as a group by creating a "How we're doing" chart to keep children accountable for their responsibilities.

- Show the children that their opinions matter by giving them choices in the work and/or decision-making. If young, keep the options to a couple, while for older kids allow for more flexibility.

- Find projects in which kids can take responsibility within their community, be it in the school, immediate surrounding community, or broader community; for instance, identify opportunities for helping the elderly, taking care of the recycling program in the school, etc.

Child Strategies

You can practice being responsible in all areas of your daily life. Here are some ideas for how to practice at home, at school, and at other activities:

- Do your chores and give your parents ideas on how you would like to help out at home.

- Practice new things you learn like setting the table or making your bed to do a good job at it.

- Do your homework and ask for help in making a checklist and being organized.

- Take care of yourself: make sure you put clean clothes on, take a daily shower, brush your teeth, comb your hair, and take out the things you will need for the next day before you go to sleep.

- In school, take pride in doing well in your assigned role in helping the class, be it door-holder or erasing the board, etc.

RESPONSIBILITY

Parent Strategies

- Make your child feel trustworthy – if you take a step back and allow your child to do something on their own, you are teaching them that they can be trusted and are capable.

- Start early – as children grow, gradually increment the chores or things they can do to contribute. Some ideas can include putting back their toys (2 years old and onward), setting the table and making their bed (5 years old onward), dressing themselves (6 years old onward), helping in the kitchen or mowing the lawn (11 years old onward), etc.

- Model how to do things, let them try it out, and give them praise and encouragement. Breathe and remember it won't be perfect and may take much longer than if you did it on your own.

- As you create a list of chores, get your child's input as to what they would like to do. Place the list where everyone can see it (family room or kitchen).

- Try to avoid nagging. Instead, allow your child to experience the consequences of not following through.

- Provide systems or kid-friendly organizers to help them reach the goal.

- Include some fun in it – with little kids, sing songs or rhymes, and with older children, allow them to make suggestions and bring a sense of humor to it.

Discussion Topics

WHAT IS RESPONSIBILITY?

A responsibility is something you must take care of or do. A responsible person is someone who can be trusted to complete their jobs or tasks. Responsibility is a life skill that is important at home, school, and play. Taking care of your responsibilities shows others that they can trust you and that you help out the people around you.

WHY ACT RESPONSIBLY?

Behaving responsibly shows others that you are mature and can be trusted, and, therefore, you are more likely to be allowed to make your own decisions. If parents and teachers can count on you to complete your work and behave in a safe manner, they are more likely to trust you to handle complicated situations. Learning responsibility is an important step in becoming an adult.

RESPONSIBILITY

Teacher's Guide to Social and Emotional Learning

DISCUSSION QUESTIONS

- What are the tasks you are responsible for at home?

- What are the tasks you are responsible for at school?

- What kind of tools can you use to make sure you take care of your responsibilities?

- What kinds of things get in the way of taking care of responsibilities?

- What could you say to a friend who is distracting you from your tasks?

- Do you wish you had more or less responsibilities? Why?

Role Play

Scenario: Emery's lunch box falls on the ground, spilling all her lunch. The lunch bell rings and she notices the janitor cleaning up her lunch.

Setting up the Scene: Please review the guidelines in the "How to use this book" section of the introduction.

Guided Questions: After the students have performed the scenario, ask the following questions *(invite both the actors and the rest of the class to answer)*:

DISCUSS FEELINGS:

- What is Emery feeling?

- What is the janitor feeling?

RESPONSIBILITY

THINKING ABOUT CHOICES:

- What do you think could happen if Emery lets the janitor clean up her mess?

- How could Emery gain by not cleaning up her mess?

- What could Emery say to the janitor to take responsibility for her actions?

- Do you think it could become a habit for Emery to ignore her responsibilities when she doesn't want to deal with something?

- What could happen if she stops being responsible?

MAKING IT PERSONAL:

Help students relate the scenario to their own lives by asking the following:

- Has a situation like this ever happened to you? What did you do?

- Is it easier to ignore your responsibilities, or to help the janitor clean up the mess? Why?

- What kinds of things do you think or say to yourself to follow through with your responsibilities?

- What are other situations similar to this where it was really hard to make a good choice (for example, doing things even if you don't want to do them)?

Teacher's Guide to Social and Emotional Learning

240

Leadership Skills

Leadership is often referred to as an individual's overall ability to motivate, inspire, or persuade a group of people to collaborate and work together towards a shared goal. When translating this into the day-to-day lives of children, it can reveal itself in a child's ability to work in a group and share their ideas in a constructive way to enhance the process; it may come out when a child can speak to the teacher assertively and share suggestions; it may be more obvious in sports as a child holds the team together and motivates others to do well in a captain role; or, in a social environment, we can see a child's leadership qualities in their friendships and through their games.

Teacher's Guide to Social and Emotional Learning

Teacher Strategies

- Learn about leaders in the classroom. As you introduce the life and work of a variety of leaders (different genders, nationalities, ethnicities, etc.), discuss what qualities they share. Discuss different types of leaders with diverse strengths and personalities. Have children connect these individuals to leaders in their own lives.

- Create leadership opportunities for different styles. Considering the strengths of your different students, offer opportunities in which each one can shine or lead in their own way. For example, with quieter or more introverted students, you can respect their style and gently help them build confidence by having them take certain roles in the class. For instance, have one of these students be in charge of taking attendance.

- Practice skills. Help children practice some important leadership skills (such as negotiation, active listening, risk-taking, communication, and empathy) through group work, scenarios, hands-on projects, service learning, etc.

Child Strategies

- Think about others and listen to them – when you work with others, take time to understand and consider what other people want and need, and how they feel. Listen without interrupting and ask questions so that they know you paid attention to what they said.

- Get out of your comfort zone – you can learn and accomplish unique things when you decide to try something new. Sometimes this might result in you taking the "road less traveled," which means you may be the first one to take this risk. For example, standing up for someone is important, but challenging when no one else is doing it.

- Pick a cause and take action. Think about what is important to you, what you value, and if there is a specific cause you believe in. Then, take action. If, for example, you are passionate about how animals are treated, then you could learn more about the issue, build a team by getting others excited to help out, think of ways to fix it, and make a plan of action.

- Set a good example. You don't have to be outgoing to be a leader; you can be a quiet and trustworthy leader by setting a good example and doing what you believe is right despite peer pressure. People will respect this.

- Accept mistakes. Mistakes are part of learning, everyone makes them, and they can be difficult to cope with at times. However, you can change a mistake into a learning opportunity by taking responsibility for what you did, apologizing, and figuring out what you would do differently.

- Build your confidence. Confidence grows when we learn to do something well or accomplish something that is difficult, so pick something you want to try from music, sports, academics, or community service and work on it so that you feel confident in your ability.

- Be a good communicator – make eye contact when talking to others, use a strong voice, learn about different topics, and share your beliefs and feelings.

- Be real. A leader is true to himself or herself and to his or her beliefs. People respect someone who is real and honest, even if they do not agree with him or her.

Parent Strategies

- Get them involved in volunteering – children develop empathy, humbleness, and respect when they learn how to give. Becoming involved in service opportunities opens the door for your children to observe, model, and practice leadership skills.

- Promote mentoring relationships with community leaders. Encourage your child to form connections with mentors such as positive athletes, artists, youth activists, team leaders, young entrepreneurs, or professionals.

- Learn about different past and current leaders – watch the news, read biographies, and discuss how these leaders affect the world and what qualities they have.

- Develop empathy – help children develop their ability to see things from another person's perspective and connect to what people may be feeling.

- Get to know your child. Although we can help children grow in their leadership style and skills, we need to do this without pushing them or expecting them to be something else. By respecting who they are, you can help your child explore his or her own strengths and provide opportunities to feel confident by learning how to do things and do a good job at them.

LEADERSHIP SKILLS

- Encourage them to make their own decisions – start by allowing them to make simple decisions as to what to wear, their hairstyle, what activities to be part of, etc.

- Practice negotiation and problem-solving. At home, leave room for negotiating certain aspects with your children or amongst siblings, such as who picks a movie to watch or what game to play. Have them practice working out a solution in which they feel is for the most part fair.

- Build resilience – praise and value the process and hard work that went into reaching a goal, not just the end product. Help them work through setbacks and persevere.

246

Discussion Topics

WHAT MAKES A GREAT LEADER?

A great leader is a person who sets a positive example and inspires others to do the same. A leader motivates others to work together toward a common goal. Strong leaders think about others and listen. They take time to understand and consider what other people want, need, and how they feel.

ARE LEADERS BORN OR MADE?

Some people are born with personality traits that make them natural leaders. However, many people become leaders through hard work or because they are passionate about a specific issue. Great leaders are not always outgoing. Many lead by quietly devoting themselves to their work and doing what they believe is right, even when they are criticized by others.

Teacher's Guide to Social and Emotional Learning

DISCUSSION QUESTIONS

- Name a famous person who you feel is or was a great leader. Why?

- Name a person from your everyday life who you feel is a good leader. Why?

- What are the qualities that make a good team captain?

- Why is it important for a leader to be a good listener?

- What should a leader do when they make a mistake?

- Why is it important for a leader to be honest?

- Do leaders need to be brave? Why?

Role Play

Scenario: Mateo is a new kid at the school and Eric has been asked by the teacher to be Mateo's "buddy."

Setting up the Scene: Please review the guidelines in the "How to use this book" section of the introduction.

Guided Questions: After the students have performed the scenario, ask the following questions *(invite both the actors and the rest of the class to answer)*:

DISCUSS FEELINGS:

- What is Eric feeling?

- What is Mateo feeling?

Teacher's Guide to Social and Emotional Learning

THINKING ABOUT CHOICES:

- What do you think could happen if Eric only hangs out with Mateo for a few minutes and then leaves him by himself?

- What would Eric gain by leaving Mateo by himself?

- How could Eric be a good buddy to Mateo?

- Do you think it could become a habit for Eric to not follow through with his role as a leader? Why?

- If this behavior became a habit for Eric, what would happen?

MAKING IT PERSONAL:

Help students relate the scenario to their own lives by asking the following:

- Has a situation like this ever happened to you? What did you do?

- Is it easier to be a leader and help the new kid, or to go and hang out with your own friends? Why?

- What kinds of things do you think or say to yourself to help you be a good leader in a situation like this?

- What are other situations similar to this where it was really hard to make a good choice and be a good leader?

LEADERSHIP SKILLS

Teacher's Guide to Social and Emotional Learning

Learning from Mistakes

"If you are not prepared to be wrong, you'll never come up with anything original," says Ken Robinson, international advisor and speaker on education, as he talks about creativity and education (Ken Robinson, "How Schools Kill Creativity." TED Conference. Feb. 2006). This perspective shares how making mistakes and transforming them into learning opportunities is a process that allows children (and adults) to develop resilience, problem-solving skills, and self-compassion. New literature in the psychology/parenting field is giving importance to letting children learn from a "scraped knee," helping reduce the anxiety, perfectionism, and lack of risk-taking that can result from being afraid of making mistakes (Wendy Mogel, "The blessing of a skinned knee: using Jewish teachings to raise self-reliant children," 2001).

Teacher Strategies

- Help children reflect on what they can do to help solve the situation and what they learned from their mistakes, both in academic and social scenarios.

- Read and discuss children's books celebrating mistakes.

- Ask open-ended questions and do more open-ended and hands-on projects that have a focus on the process rather than the end-result.

- Share your mistakes and the lessons learned from them.

- Encourage children to share and reflect on mistakes.

Child Strategies

Parents should go over these questions and concepts with their child.

- Change your mistake into a learning opportunity. Making mistakes can be hard but are also a great way of learning something new, so think, "What could I do different next time?"

- Admit to your mistakes – people will trust and respect you when you accept responsibility for a mistake.

- If someone was hurt by your mistake, think of how you can make them feel better.

- Ask your parents about a time they made a mistake and how they fixed it.

- Be kind to yourself by saying to yourself, "It is OK to make mistakes; I can learn from this."

 Teacher's Guide to Social and Emotional Learning

Parent Strategies

- Let your child know that you don't expect him/her to be perfect.

- Reassure him/her that your love is unconditional, regardless of their mistakes or errors in judgment.

- Don't try to solve your child's mistakes and avoid the natural consequences that may come. Instead, focus on the solution.

- Provide examples of your own mistakes, the consequences, and how you learned from them. You can model the process of bouncing back from mistakes and promoting resilience.

- Encourage them to take responsibility for their mistakes and not blame others.

- Praise them for their efforts when overcoming setbacks.

- Mentor them on how to apologize when their mistakes have hurt others.

256

Discussion Topics

WHAT DO WE LEARN FROM MISTAKES?

Everyone makes mistakes; they are a simple fact of life. Mistakes can be hard, but they are also a great way of learning something new. When something doesn't go the way you had planned, you can always try it in a different way. When you understand what went wrong the first time, you will be able to make a better choice the second time around. Using mistakes as a chance to learn helps you to grow and do things better in the future.

WHY ADMIT MISTAKES?

It is important to admit when you make a mistake. People will trust and respect you more when you take responsibility for your mistakes. If someone was hurt by your mistake, talk with them about how you can fix it and how you can help them feel better.

Teacher's Guide to Social and Emotional Learning

DISCUSSION QUESTIONS

- Share a time when you made a mistake.

- Is it easy or difficult to admit when you have made a mistake?

- Share a time when a mistake turned out to be a good thing.

- Have you ever seen an adult make a mistake? How did they handle it?

- What advice would you give to a friend who has made a mistake?

- What is something you have learned from a mistake?

Role Play

Scenario: Antonio's teacher assigned him the role of class gardener. Antonio forgot his responsibility and now some of the plants are dead.

Setting up the Scene: Please review the guidelines in the "How to use this book" section of the introduction.

Guided Questions: After the students have performed the scenario, ask the following questions *(invite both the actors and the rest of the class to answer)*:

DISCUSS FEELINGS:

- What is Antonio feeling?

- What is Antonio's teacher feeling?

THINKING ABOUT CHOICES:

- What do you think could happen if Antonio doesn't talk to the teacher but waters the plants a lot to try to revive them?

- What would Antonio gain by over-watering the plants and not talking to his teacher?

- How could Antonio acknowledge and try to fix his mistake?

- Do you think it could become a habit for Antonio to not admit or learn from his mistakes? Why?

MAKING IT PERSONAL:

Help students relate the scenario to their own lives by asking the following:

- Has a situation like this ever happened to you? What did you do?

- Is it easier to try to cover your mistake and over-water the plants, or is it easier to explain what happened to the teacher and make a reminder for yourself to water the plants in the future? Why?

- What kinds of things do you think or say to yourself to help you acknowledge your mistake?

- What are other situations similar to this where it was really hard to make a good choice and learn from your mistakes?

Teacher's Guide to Social and Emotional Learning

Manners & Respect

Teaching our children manners is as important as any other academic or formal instruction. Social civility allows us to establish relationships and build communities; it provides guidelines to our interactions and creates a framework based on our social and cultural traditions. In teaching our children and helping to build their characters, we consistently return to the guiding values of respect, consideration, and honesty.

Manners are taught continually through example in our day-to-day relations. Parents, teachers, family, and strangers help instill awareness to the needs of others and help model the power of language and actions in building relationships and community. Children learn to communicate assertively with respect and kindness and see that their choices impact others, reinforcing the importance of balancing their personal needs with the needs of those around them.

Teacher Strategies

- Brainstorm why it matters – discuss with children about why manners matter and how they help build the classroom and school community.

- Encourage the "magic words" – model and reinforce the use of words like "thank you" and "please" in your classroom.

- Practice greeting others – practice how to make eye contact by shaking hands while greeting someone by name during morning circle. For example, ask a child to turn to the peer on his right, make eye contact and, while shaking hands, ask, "Hi, Sue, what did you do this weekend?" and go around the circle asking and answering the question. You can also model this gesture as each child comes into the classroom during the morning.

- Practice "I" statements to solve problems. Teaching steps and words to use when working out problems helps children build tools on how to respectfully address a variety of situations.

- Weave manners into the curriculum – find a creative way in which to teach a variety of character-building skills as part of a holistic view of education.

264

Child Strategies

- Remember the power of words. The way you speak to others can help fix problems, make someone feel good, and build relationships. Simple words can make a big difference; "please" changes a bossy command into a kind request, "thank you" makes someone feel appreciated, and an honest "sorry" resolves even the most difficult of problems.

- A smile makes the difference – greeting others with a friendly smile is a friendly way to start talking to them.

- Make eye contact and look at the person you are speaking to. This is a way to show both respect and that you are listening to them.

- Speak clearly – be careful not to mumble when you talk. Practice with friends and parents to feel more confident in speaking clearly.

- Greet people by name. Learning people's names and saying them when you say "hi" or talk to the person will make him or her feel special.

- Say "No" nicely. Being respectful does not mean you have to always agree to everything someone asks you to do. You can say "No" in a graceful and respectful way, saying, "I am sorry, but I cannot help that day since I have a basketball game at the same time" or, "I can't go to your house, but maybe we can play at recess."

 Teacher's Guide to Social and Emotional Learning

Parent Strategies

- Values and manners begin at home. Model for your child and reinforce courtesy, respect, and humbleness as a way to set the foundation for important social and emotional skills.

- Simple exchanges are powerful. Teaching your child how to make eye contact and greet someone, to say "Please" and "Thank you," to hold the door, or let an elder have their seat are all gestures that foster gratitude, empathy, and compassion.

- Promote good sportsmanship. As important as drive is in competition, so is fair play. When parents show fairness, treat their children and others with kindness, and value collaboration as well as individuality, they will be teaching their children through their actions.

- Interrupting is not OK – starting at a young age, it is important children learn not to interrupt. Gently ask them to wait until you finish your conversation, which teaches them that this is also a way of respecting someone else's time.

266

Discussion Topics

WHAT ARE MANNERS?

Manners are actions and ways of behaving that are accepted as being polite. They tell us how to act in different situations to be respectful of others. Manners change depending on the culture, and we learn manners through our daily interactions with those around us.

WHY DO WE USE THEM?

Manners can be used as a sign of respect and a way of showing kindness. When someone uses good manners, it shows that they care about other people, and that they are part of a community that has an accepted way of treating one another. Good manners help us to have good relationships with others.

Teacher's Guide to Social and Emotional Learning

DISCUSSION QUESTIONS

- What are some examples of manners used when meeting someone for the first time?

- What are some examples of manners used when speaking on the phone?

- What is an example of a polite way to refuse something?

- Why is it important to learn and use people's names?

- Why are good manners important at school?

- What are some common manners we use in our daily lives? (Examples: waiting in line for your turn, raising a hand to speak in class, saying "please" and "thank you," etc.)

- What would happen if no one used good manners?

Role Play

Scenario: Finley is on a play date at Charlotte's house. Charlotte's mom has cooked fish for lunch, which Finley does not like.

Setting up the Scene: Please review the guidelines in the "How to use this book" section of the introduction.

Guided Questions: After the students have performed the scenario, ask the following questions *(invite both the actors and the rest of the class to answer)*:

DISCUSS FEELINGS:

- What is Finley feeling?

- What is Charlotte's mom feeling?

Teacher's Guide to Social and Emotional Learning

THINKING ABOUT CHOICES:

- What do you think could happen if Finley refuses to eat his lunch and tells Charlotte that fish is yucky?

- How would it benefit Finley to not politely share why he doesn't like fish?

- What could Finley say or do to show good manners?

- Do you think it could become a habit for Finley to be rude when someone gives him something that he dislikes? What could happen if it becomes a habit?

MAKING IT PERSONAL:

Help students relate the scenario to their own lives by asking the following:

- Has a situation like this ever happened to you? What did you do?

- Is it easier to make rude comments and not eat your lunch, or to politely try a few bites and request something different if you still don't enjoy it? Why?

- What kinds of things do you think or say to yourself to help you make a good choice and show respect in a situation like this?

- What are other situations similar to this where it was really hard to make a good choice (for example, using good manners and acting respectfully)?

MANNERS & RESPECT

Negotiating

Negotiating is an important life skill that develops at an early age as children work out day-to-day situations with siblings or friends when deciding which game to play and with parents when deciding what to wear. It is about having a dialogue in order to reach a compromise. As children grow, their negotiating toolkit develops and becomes more sophisticated. Their initial problem-solving skills, such as taking turns with a toy when playing with a sibling, later on become more complex when in group work they assign tasks based on their own strengths and interests.

Negotiating is a process of communication which can empower a child to both clarify and share their opinions and feelings on a given situation and listen to another's view. Therefore, in practicing this ability children develop empathy, perspective taking, and assertiveness. Having opportunities in which a child can negotiate in a way that feels fair and which results favorably for those involved will increase a sense of confidence and an understanding of their own and other people's needs, wants, and limits.

Teacher Strategies

Help students build skills they can use to resolve conflicts and negotiate by creating opportunities to practice them:

- Give students a problem and ask them to state what they would propose and support their suggestion using "I" statements. For instance, "I think it would be a good idea if we play tag because everyone can play the game" or "I suggest we come up with four activities so that everyone can choose what they want to play."

- Do active-listening activities. Pair students to share something (such as what they did for the summer); one is the listener who will repeat the words back to the speaker and ask if they understood, and then they switch places.

- Do a brainstorming session with the class about options to solve a situation. For instance, how could they decide when there is a disagreement about who is out in four square?

- When students are working in groups, help them reflect on what worked well when working together and what things they could have done differently. Ask them how they arrived at group agreements – did some quit trying? Did someone impose the final decision? Did they find a joint solution?

Child Strategies

- Whether you and your friends are trying to pick which movie to watch or what game to play during recess, remember that you can find a solution that everyone feels is for the most part fair, even if the solution was not your first choice.

- Here are the steps you can follow:

    1. Decide what you want.

    2. Listen to what others want.

    3. Brainstorm ideas for how you can decide (taking turns, playing Roshambo, taking a vote, working out an agreement).

    4. Agree on a solution for all.

    5. Put your plan in action.

Teacher's Guide to Social and Emotional Learning

Parent Strategies

- Help your child start with the right mindset. Teach children that negotiation can be a win-win situation, and that there is not one way of winning only.

- Guide your child in generating and evaluating different solutions, such as, "Let's think of three ways that we could do this differently."

- Ask them to take another's perspective: "What do you think your friend would like to do?"

- Model flexibility. When negotiating with your child during day-to-day situations, model how you can come up with different possibilities and adapt to a variety of solutions.

- If your child gets upset or frustrated, clarify the rules and boundaries of the negotiation: "If we are going to choose what movie to watch, we all need to hear each other so we need to keep our voices down," or, if needed, offer some options in which they can calm down (for instance, taking a break and coming back).

Discussion Topics

WHAT IS NEGOTIATION?

Negotiation is a tool used to deal with conflict in which a person or group shares their opinions and feelings about a situation and then listens to the other person or group's point of view. After each side has shared their opinions, everyone works together to find a way to make both sides happy. Negotiation often means having to give up some of your needs in order to have your most important needs met.

WHY USE NEGOTIATION?

The ability to negotiate is an important life skill people use in their personal relationships, as well as at school and work. Conflict cannot always be avoided, and knowing how to deal with conflict through tools like negotiation helps you to fix problems without hurting your relationships.

Teacher's Guide to Social and Emotional Learning

DISCUSSION QUESTIONS

- Share a time when you used negotiation to deal with a conflict.

- Share a time when you experienced a conflict and did not use negotiation.

- Why is it important to find a solution that everyone feels is fair?

- Why is it sometimes necessary to give up something you want in a negotiation?

- What are some simple and fast ways to deal with conflict? Are they a type of negotiation? (Examples: taking turns, taking a vote).

- Give some examples of situations at school that might require negotiation (Examples: who gets to be team captain, rules of a game, and individual jobs in a group assignment).

278

Role Play

Scenario: Dexter wants to play a new sport this year, but his parents say he has to give up a sport he plays now before he adds a new one. He doesn't want to give up any of the sports he plays now.

Setting up the Scene: Please review the guidelines in the "How to use this book" section of the introduction.

Guided Questions: After the students have performed the scenario, ask the following questions *(invite both the actors and the rest of the class to answer)*:

DISCUSS FEELINGS:

- What is Dexter feeling?

- What are Dexter's parents feeling?

THINKING ABOUT CHOICES:

- What do you think could happen if Dexter tells his parents that if he can't play the new sport, he will stop working hard at school?

- What would Dexter gain by getting upset or being rude to his parents?

- How could Dexter negotiate with his parents so that he can try the new sport?

- Do you think it could become a habit for Dexter to complain or be rude unless he gets his way? What could happen if it becomes a habit?

MAKING IT PERSONAL:

Help students relate the scenario to their own lives by asking the following:

- Has a situation like this ever happened to you? What did you do?

- Is it easier to be angry when you don't get what you want or to talk things through? Why?

- What kinds of things do you think or say to yourself to help you figure out a fair way to solve problems?

- What are other situations similar to this where it was really hard to make a good choice (for example, negotiating when arguments arise)?

Patience

You may have heard of Stanford University's well-known "Marshmallow Experiment" which examined the idea of delayed gratification (Mischel, Walter; Ebbesen, Ebbe B.; Raskoff Zeiss, Antonette, "Cognitive and attentional mechanisms in delay of gratification," Feb. 1972). This mainly refers to the ability to have patience and self-control, resisting the temptation of an immediate reward to be able to wait for a more enduring and meaningful reward, which will come later. In this experiment, a marshmallow was offered to each child participating and if they could resist from eating it immediately, they were promised two instead of one. The scientists arrived at the conclusion that waiting longer was an indicator of future success as they analyzed data and followed the children's development through time. This simple experiment shed light as to how coping with life's stress, adversity, and frustrations help us develop resilience and grit.

     Teacher's Guide to Social and Emotional Learning

Teacher Strategies

- Talk to kids about how it is hard to wait and have them share times they had to be patient and how they managed (waiting at a doctor's office, not getting dessert until after supper, waiting for a game to arrive, etc.).

- Reinforce classroom routines like taking turns, circle time, and listening to others to discuss how these develop patience and respect.

- Do long-term projects with intermediate steps and internal incentives that allow students to stretch their ability to wait for closure and discuss the process.

- Introduce tools like "pause buttons" and "stop and think," and use visual and physical reminders.

- Play games in which kids have to show self-control before getting to the desired reward.

Child Strategies

- Slow down and take a deep breath if you feel you are getting upset or frustrated.

- Have a quiet space to calm down, figure out how you are feeling, and say it out loud. Start by saying, "I am tired of waiting," and then say to yourself "I can wait" or "It's OK, I can calm down."

- Find something to do while you are waiting. Let's say you have finished your work and need to wait while others finish… you might be able to read, draw, or look around the classroom and pay attention to the different things on the walls.

- Make a plan. If something seems too big to do, like a project or homework, ask for help on how to make it into smaller steps and go one by one.

- Make plans for the future – for instance, think of something you want to get (like a great toy) and, with your parents, come up with steps and a future date to get it.

- Remember that everyone is fast and slow at different things. You can show your patience with your younger siblings or classmates by not yelling or getting frustrated.

PATIENCE

Parent Strategies

- Be OK with letting your child become more tolerant of discomfort. Allow room for healthy frustration by not fixing things for him/her or giving in to your child's immediate demands.

- Help them develop coping strategies. Check off days on the calendar and brainstorm things they can do while they wait to help them keep in mind that the discomfort is temporary. One way is to acknowledge their effort, saying "I know it is hard to wait, and you are doing a great job in being patient."

- Keep expectations reasonable based on your child's age.

- Recognize and reward their ability in waiting for something. One practical way can be through helping them think about how they use their allowance and exploring the difference between getting something they immediately desire vs. a plan to get something more meaningful that will give them more satisfaction. Celebrate their success.

Discussion Topics

WHAT IS PATIENCE?

Patience is the ability to stay calm while waiting for something. When people learn to deal with the stress and frustration of having to wait, they develop the strength to handle other difficult situations.

IT PAYS TO WAIT.

It's hard to wait, but sometimes using patience while working toward a goal can result in a bigger reward. For example, an impatient person might spend their weekly allowance on small items that last a short period of time, like a treat or a game at an arcade. A patient person, on the other hand, might save a portion, or even their entire allowance, over a long period of time with the goal of purchasing an expensive item that can be enjoyed over and over, like a video game, a piece of clothing, or even a cell phone or computer.

PATIENCE

DISCUSSION QUESTIONS

- Share a time when you used patience to work toward a goal.

- Share a time when impatience got the better of you.

- What are some things you can do to calm down when feeling impatient?

- What are some things you can do to distract yourself when feeling impatient?

- What would you say to a friend who is having a hard time waiting for something?

- Without using names, give an example of a time when you had to be patient when dealing with another person.

Role Play

Scenario: Will loves skateboarding, but he is not that good. Will's parents have asked him to make time to practice.

Setting up the Scene: Please review the guidelines in the "How to use this book" section of the introduction.

Guided Questions: After the students have performed the scenario, ask the following questions *(invite both the actors and the rest of the class to answer)*:

DISCUSS FEELINGS:

- What is Will feeling?

- What are Will's parents feeling?

Teacher's Guide to Social and Emotional Learning

THINKING ABOUT CHOICES:

- What do you think could happen if Will gives up and decides to try another hobby that is easy to learn?

- How could Will benefit from choosing a different, easier hobby?

- What could Will do to stop getting frustrated and be patient with skateboarding?

- Do you think it could become a habit for Will to give up whenever he gets impatient? What could happen if impatience becomes a habit?

290

MAKING IT PERSONAL:

Help students relate the scenario to their own lives by asking the following:

- Has a situation like this ever happened to you? What did you do?

- Is it easier to choose a different, easier hobby, or is it easier to be patient while you continue learning how to skateboard? Why?

- What kinds of things do you think or say to yourself to help you make a good choice and persevere when things get challenging?

- What are other situations similar to this where it was really hard to make a good choice (for example, when you want to give up or get frustrated or impatient)?

Teacher's Guide to Social and Emotional Learning

Self-Awareness

Teacher's Guide to Social and Emotional Learning

294

Appropriate vs. Inappropriate Physical Contact

Our relationship with our own body is dynamic and changes throughout our lives. It is a constant process in which we form our self-image and sense of self as we figure out our personal space and our boundaries, become attuned with our senses, and integrate the images of how others see us with the ones we have formed. Through touch and movement we develop a connection with our body and learn self-care, safety, and respect. Touch is a wonderful part of human relationships and it is essential to healthy human development. At the same time, it is important to teach children about safe touch and personal boundaries at different times in their development.

Curiosity about the body is normal and it is helpful to provide children and youth with age-appropriate resources about how the body works, body changes, puberty, sexuality, and abuse prevention. Starting at a young age, it is important to discuss with children how their body belongs to them, and that they can decide how they interact with others (for instance, when playing

Teacher's Guide to Social and Emotional Learning

with other children and when with adults or with strangers). Children need to define their personal space (an imaginary bubble around them) and respect others' space. Safe touch can be explained to little ones by pointing out that no one should touch them in the body areas covered by a bathing suit (clarifying how a doctor can do so when parents are present). As children become older, the concept of physical boundaries and emotional boundaries can be discussed in conjunction with practicing assertiveness when someone crosses those boundaries.

Teacher Strategies

- Read age-appropriate books with the kids in your class on the subject.

- Have class discussions about words and phrases they can use if they feel uncomfortable with the way someone is touching them.

- Initiate games with the children to pretend they have bubbles around them, and to share how far their bubbles extend from their bodies—encourage the students to respect each other's personal bubbles.

- Teach children how to be assertive and use confident language to describe how they think and feel in class.

APPROPRIATEVS.INAPPROPRIATEPHYSICALCONTACT

Teacher's Guide to Social and Emotional Learning

Child Strategies

Parents should go over these concepts and questions with children.

- Remember your body belongs to you.

- If someone is playing too rough or is not respecting your personal space, you can say, "Please move. I need more space."

- If you feel uncomfortable with the way someone is touching you (someone hugs you too tight, pinches you, pokes you, or touches your body in an area that your bathing suit usually covers), you should tell them to stop and move away before telling an adult you trust.

- If someone is asking you to do something you do not want to do (play a game or do something you don't feel is OK), you can say you don't want to, move away, and tell an adult you trust.

298

Parent Strategies

- Teach your children to express their feelings.

- Talk to them about personal space and safety.

- Practice examples of sentences that they could use to advocate for their personal space, in case they were in a situation that might be too close for their comfort. For instance, "Don't take that; I'm using it right now," or, "Please move over; you're standing too close to me."

- Help set personal boundaries at home; for instance, teaching children to close the door when they are in the bathroom or bedroom or when they are getting dressed or undressed.

- Provide age-appropriate books about personal space, safe boundaries, and abuse prevention.

299   Teacher's Guide to Social and Emotional Learning

Discussion Topics

Parents should go over these concepts and questions with children.

WHAT IS APPROPRIATE PHYSICAL CONTACT?

Your body belongs to you, and it is up to you to decide how to use it to interact with others in a safe way. This means determining your personal space and boundaries. Physical contact with others is part of healthy relationships, as long as the contact is safe, respectful, and does not make either person feel uncomfortable. The amount of physical contact that you are comfortable with is likely to depend on your relationship with the other person. For example, while you may feel comfortable hugging a friend or family member, you might not feel comfortable hugging someone you have just met.

WHAT IS INAPPROPRIATE PHYSICAL CONTACT?

Inappropriate physical contact is any kind of touch that makes you feel unsafe, uncomfortable, or that crosses the imaginary boundary that you have determined as your personal space.

DISCUSSION QUESTIONS

- What are some examples of appropriate physical contact?

- What are some examples of inappropriate physical contact that you have witnessed at school?

- What can you say to someone who is invading your personal space?

- Who can you talk to if someone is invading your personal space and will not stop?

- A trusted adult can help you if someone is or has made inappropriate physical contact with you. Who are the trusted adults in your life?

Role Play

Scenario: Jia's friend Libby always elbows her whenever she makes a joke. Jia really does not like it.

Setting up the Scene: Please review the guidelines in the "How to use this book" section of the introduction.

Guided Questions: After the students have performed the scenario, ask the following questions *(invite both the actors and the rest of the class to answer)*:

DISCUSS FEELINGS:

- What is Jia feeling?

- What is Libby feeling?

THINKING ABOUT CHOICES:

- What do you think could happen if Jia does nothing?

- What would Jia gain by doing nothing?

- What could Jia do to set boundaries between her and Libby?

- Do you think that it could become a habit for Jia to not tell others when she needs some space? Why?

MAKING IT PERSONAL:

Help students relate the scenario to their own lives by asking the following:

- Has a situation like this ever happened to you? What did you do?

- Is it easier to stand up for yourself or do nothing in a situation like this? Why?

- What kinds of things do you think or say to yourself to help you set boundaries in this type of situation?

- Have you experienced other situations similar to this (where it was hard to stand up for yourself and explain to others about appropriate physical contact)? What happened?

APPROPRIATE VS. INAPPROPRIATE PHYSICAL CONTACT

Dealing with Bullies

A great definition of bullying for kids comes from stopbullying.gov which states, "Bullying is unwanted, aggressive behavior among school aged children that involves a real or perceived power imbalance. The behavior is repeated, or has the potential to be repeated, over time. Bullying includes actions such as making threats, spreading rumors, attacking someone physically or verbally, and excluding someone from a group on purpose." Bullying is not a single or random situation of exclusion, meanness, teasing, or aggression. This can help distinguish bullying from peer pressure or teasing which can be addressed with other approaches.

Types of bullying include physical (hitting, kicking, or pinching), verbal (insults, intimidation, being racist, sexist, or homophobic), emotional (spreading rumors, humiliating, mimicking, or hurting someone's reputation), and cyber bullying (harassment online or in texting, flaming, exclusion, or masquerading).

Bullying is a serious issue affecting youth at different ages and from a diversity of backgrounds, and a thoughtful and necessary response requires a joint effort of parents, educators, institutions, and community members.

 Teacher's Guide to Social and Emotional Learning

Teacher Strategies

- Take it seriously. If a child, parent, or another person shares that someone is being bullied, take it seriously and take steps to respond.

- Intervene immediately. If the situation just occurred, make sure everyone is safe and separate the students.

- Listen and support – work closely with the child who is being bullied to provide reassurance, support, and care. Let them know it is not their fault and that you will work with the child, parents, and the school to help him or her feel safe.

- Gather information – in a gentle and calm way, find out when, where, and how the incident(s) occurred, and who was involved and present. Talk to the students separately to gather information.

- Get others involved. Work closely with the principal and school counselor to explore how the school can respond accordingly.

- Work with the parents. Share the incident with the child's family and work closely to provide support and a follow-up plan.

- Be proactive through education on prevention. One of the most important ways to reduce bullying is through education. Tap into resources on bullying and do activities to brainstorm, discuss, and learn about bullying and how to address it.

Child Strategies

- No one should be bullied – if you find yourself in a situation where you feel someone is bullying you, remember that it is never your fault and no one deserves to be treated that way.

- You are not alone. Let an adult know, as they can often do something so the situation does not escalate. It is really important you do talk to the school counselor, a parent, or someone you trust to help you feel better.

- Use the buddy system. Avoid being with a bully on your own by asking a friend to accompany you to the places you may encounter the bully. Do the same for your friend.

- Don't respond with aggression – if you fight back, the conflict will probably escalate further. Instead, avoid the bully, walk away, or try to act unimpressed.

- If a friend is being bullied, tell the bully to stop; do not join in even if you are afraid. Try to comfort the person who is bullied, or tell an adult.

- If you are cyber bullied, do not respond to the message (even if you are angry or upset). Save the message, block or delete the sender, report the situation to the website, and tell an adult. Avoid social networks that allow for people to make anonymous comments about you.

Parent Strategies

- Support your child. Sometimes one of the hardest things for children to do is to tell an adult that they are being bullied. Thus, if your child shares this, listen calmly, be supportive, and reassure them that it is not their fault. Let them know they did the right thing in coming to you.

- Find out what happened. As you have a conversation about the incident(s), note when and where it happened, if there is a history of similar incidents, who was involved, and if anyone else has witnessed it. If there is any cyber bullying, do not delete the messages so that you can show them to the school or the appropriate people.

- Work with the school. Talk to the teacher, principal, or school counselor and work with them to create a plan of action in which your child's safety will be ensured. It is recommended that you work through the school so that they can work with the parents of the child who is bullying, rather than contacting the family directly, as this may escalate the situation further.

Discussion Topics

WHAT IS BULLYING?

Bullying is when someone intentionally and repeatedly causes physical or emotional harm to another person who feels like they cannot fight back. Bullying is not a single or random incident of meanness or teasing. These situations are considered bullying when they happen over and over again.

WHAT DOES BULLYING LOOK LIKE?

Bullying can be physical, like hitting, kicking, or pinching. It can be verbal, such as insults, intimidation, or offensive comments. Bullying can be emotional, through spreading rumors, humiliating, mimicking, or hurting someone's reputation. A popular form of bullying today is cyber bullying, which is harassment online or via text.

DISCUSSION QUESTIONS

- Share a time when you experienced bullying.

- Have you ever witnessed bullying?

- Why do some people feel afraid to speak up when they witness bullying?

- What advice would you give to a friend who is being bullied?

- Who can you talk to if someone is bullying you?

- What actions can you take if you are being cyber bullied?

- Do you think there should be consequences to cyber bullying? If so, what should they be?

Role Play

Scenario: Katie got hurt while playing soccer with a group of kids. The group of kids made a mean comment: "You really suck at this." When she got upset, they said "SORRY," as if they did not mean it.

Setting up the Scene: Please review the guidelines in the "How to use this book" section of the introduction.

Guided Questions: After the students have performed the scenario, ask the following questions *(invite both the actors and the rest of the class to answer)*:

DISCUSS FEELINGS:

- What is Katie feeling?

- What is the group of kids feeling?

Teacher's Guide to Social and Emotional Learning

THINKING ABOUT CHOICES:

- What do you think could happen if Katie ignores the other kids?

- What would Katie gain by ignoring the other kids?

- What should Katie do in response to the mean comment?

- What could happen if Katie complains to the coach?

- Do you think that either ignoring the other kids or complaining to an adult could become a habit, and something that Katie might start doing every time she gets made fun of? What could happen if it becomes a habit?

MAKING IT PERSONAL:

Help students relate the scenario to their own lives by asking the following:

- Has a situation like this ever happened to you? What did you do?

- In a situation like this, would it be easier to ignore the other kids or tell everyone that teasing is not cool? Why?

- What kinds of things do you think or say to yourself to help you make a good choice when you're dealing with bullies?

- What are other situations like this where it was really hard to make a good choice (for example, needing to decide between ignoring someone and standing up for yourself)?

Teacher's Guide to Social and Emotional Learning

314

Following Rules & Reporting

ollowing Rules: Elementary-age children look to adults for clear, defined rules that set boundaries and limits with little room for ambiguity. At school, teachers could take time at the beginning of the school year to discuss school rules and classroom rules. At home, parents could specifically discuss rules related to chores and expected behaviors and discuss safety issues.

Boundaries are not just important as a way to create a safe environment for all; they also have an important psychological function. As children explore, test, and define boundaries, they also organize and internally shape their own way of understanding the world and their place within it. Healthy boundaries and limits help create both internal and external order. They help with emotional regulation and impulsivity. Finally, and very importantly, boundaries also allow children to gain a clearer sense of themselves in relation to others as they create healthy relationships and learn to take care of their bodies and their emotions.

Reporting vs. Tattling: Tattling is a way in which children figure out how to deal with their social and inner worlds. For teachers and parents, it can sometimes be frustrating and time-consuming to manage "tattling," but understanding the developmental reasons why this may be happening can be helpful in guiding the children to develop other ways to cope with their environment. Some of the reasons for tattling may be:

- The child may have a real concern and feel the adult needs to know.

- The child does not yet have the social skills to deal with the situation and may need some guidance in what to say or do in specific situations.

- Elementary children are refining their inner moral compass, and thus rules and what is right/wrong/fair is very important to them. Their tools are still quite inflexible and inexperienced, thus at the elementary stage children can be highly critical and rigid in their expectations and understanding of rules.

- Children will be testing limits and rules as a way to understand their own boundaries and behaviors. Interestingly, some children will learn this not by exploring the limits themselves, but by observing others and "tattling" to figure out what the adult's response is.

- Tattling may be a way in which a child is gaining attention and wants to be acknowledged for following the rules, thus they try to get this type of affirmation.

As adults, it is important to find a balance to create a safe environment in which the child can deal with some difficulties and does not feel they should tattle all the time, but, at the same time, knows that they can tell an adult if something important is happening.

Teacher Strategies

Following Rules:

- Create rules with your class. In the beginning of the year, guide the students so that they can be part of creating the classroom rules and expectations. The children can then sign the shared contract. This way the children feel more connected and responsible for following the rules.

- Have simple rules.

- Teachers will benefit from reminding students of school rules and consequences for not following rules.

- Discuss expected classroom behavior. Inform students when you can be interrupted during class time.

- Provide an open communication for children to come up and discuss issues with you.

When rules are broken:

- Discuss the situation in private with all parties involved.

- Calm down and make sure you hear your students.

- Let children know when it is OK to tattle and when students have to work it out.

Reporting vs. Tattling:

- Set the expectations of tattling in the beginning of the year by brainstorming with the group about situations that would either fall into "tell an adult," "you can handle yourself," and "let it go." This way, it may be clearer for children to determine what they should do and teachers can clarify and reinforce through the year the reflection of what type of "problem" a situation may fall under as things arise.

- Teach problem-solving skills and practice the language they can use to address different situations by themselves.

- Validate when a child shares a difficulty that needed to be brought to your attention. When it is something that they can handle or let go of, give a respectful and simple response or affirmation and help them figure out what things they can do.

- Offer different ways in which kids can get positive attention in case tattling has become their way to look for attention. For instance, they can have a unique role in the class, or you may decide with the child a nonverbal signal, like a nod, to affirm when they have handled an issue on their own or have let go. This way you support their increasing social skills.

Child Strategies

Parents should go over these concepts and questions with children.

Following Rules:

- If you feel you are not sure of a classroom rule, ask your teacher during a quiet time such as recess.

- When you are in doubt about a family rule, ask your parent before engaging in any activity that might be against family rules.

Reporting vs. Tattling:

- Think about whether this is "something an adult should know," "something I can handle," or "something I can let go."

- If it is a problem in which someone is getting hurt, you should go and tell an adult.

- If someone is doing something you don't like, in a clear tone you can use a phrase like, "I want you to stop" or move away from the situation. If this does not work, then you can tell an adult and let them know that you already tried to work this out and you need more help.

- There are times that you can "let go" (for example, someone is using the colored pencil you wanted, but you can choose another one), so think about the problem and whether it is something you can "let go." Don't worry about these problems!

Parent Strategies

Following Rules:

- Talk to your children about expected behavior around the house, such as rules around chores e.g. everyone must put their dirty laundry in the hamper, their dishes in the sink after a meal, etc.

- Discuss rules around talking to strangers or neighbors.

- Discuss emergency plans and emergency contact info.

- Discuss rules around social media usage.

- Compliment good behavior.

- When rules are not followed, impose developmentally-sound consequences such as time-outs for younger children and loss of privileges for older children.

- Logical consequences directly related to the behavior can be effective as they teach children that there are natural consequences that may come from their behaviors. For instance, if the child spilled the milk, they clean up the table.

Teacher's Guide to Social and Emotional Learning

Reporting vs. Tattling:

- Find a good balance between banning tattling and encouraging it by reinforcing it in every situation.

- Help your child figure out where a specific situation may fall under "tell an adult," "you can handle yourself," or "let it go."

- Help your child develop strategies and language to deal with life's setbacks.

- Be careful with jumping in or solving a problem too quickly when one of your children tattles. Find out more about the situation (to see if it is something you need to address or they can handle it on their own), tone your response down to avoid reinforcing the tattling, and see if together you can come up with solutions.

Discussion Topics

WHAT ARE RULES?

A rule is an instruction that guides how you should behave or act. Rules are created to make sure that people are safe and can take care of their responsibilities. There are different rules for different situations, including, for example, classroom rules and home rules.

WHAT IF SOMEONE IS BREAKING THE RULES?

Often when people witness someone breaking the rules, they feel that they must report this to someone in charge. It is important to get help from an adult or authority figure if someone is in danger of being hurt or if you do not know how to handle the situation. However, as you get older and can recognize what should be happening in a given situation, you can often encourage others to follow the rules without the help of an adult.

DISCUSSION QUESTIONS

- What are some rules that you have to follow at home? What happens if you do not follow them?

- What are some rules that you have to follow at school? What happens if you do not follow them?

- Do adults have to follow rules? What are some examples?

- What should you do if you see someone breaking a rule and you are afraid they may get hurt?

- What is the difference between getting help and "tattling"?

- What should you do if you are confused about a rule at home or at school?

Role Play

Scenario: Adam sits next to Freddie and Freddie is always making funny noises. In the middle of a test, Freddie makes a strange noise with his armpits and Adam can't help but laugh. The teacher is angry and asks what is going on.

Setting up the Scene: Please review the guidelines in the "How to use this book" section of the introduction.

Guided Questions: After the students have performed the scenario, ask the following questions *(invite both the actors and the rest of the class to answer)*:

DISCUSS FEELINGS:

- What is Adam feeling?

- What is the teacher feeling?

Teacher's Guide to Social and Emotional Learning

THINKING ABOUT CHOICES:

- What do you think could happen if Adam says he does not know or if he says that Freddie made the noise?

- How would it benefit Adam to lie or blame someone else?

- What should Adam say to the teacher to do the right thing?

- Do you think that it could become a habit for Adam to not follow class rules or blame others when he gets in trouble? What could happen if it becomes a habit?

MAKING IT PERSONAL:

Help students relate the scenario to their own lives by asking the following:

- Has a situation like this ever happened to you? What did you do?

- In a situation like this, would it be easier to lie, blame someone else, or apologize? Why?

- What kinds of things do you think or say to yourself to help you make a good choice when it comes to following rules and reporting?

- What are other situations like this where it was really hard to make a good choice (for example, if someone is behaving badly or isn't following the rules)?

Teacher's Guide to Social and Emotional Learning

Minding My Own Business

Our society greatly values privacy, and yet we also live a contrasting world of sharing and oversharing of information through media and social networks. Perhaps it is our innate need to feel connected to others, our intrinsic curiosity, or our need to gather and give meaning to information, but the fact is, we are constant detectives of what is happening around us.

Nonetheless, as natural inquirers we also learn through time that there are limits to how we gather information and what we do with it, thus creating our compass of ethics, respect, and good manners. We figure out that boundaries are crucial not only to protect someone else's privacy, but also to guard our own personal space (be it physical, social, or emotional) so that we can form our self-definition and develop our ability for self-reflection. Thus, as we grow, we practice how to set our boundaries and work on balancing the need to know about others, while reminding ourselves when to mind our own business.

Teacher's Guide to Social and Emotional Learning

Teacher Strategies

- Brainstorm with children about situations in which it is OK to get involved or get someone else involved, and when it is not their business.

- Teach children to stop and think, "Does this have anything to do with me? Do I need to be involved?" before they decide to jump in.

- Help children set their boundaries – come up with ways in which they can politely tell others to mind their own business. For instance, "I appreciate you worry about me, but I want to figure this out on my own," or, "Thanks for listening. I needed to vent, but I am not sure I want advice right now."

- Help children reflect on the importance of respect. Based on the age of your students, come up with scenarios and guiding questions that can help discern the subtleties of gossip, minding your own business, and tattling, and how to have a clearer sense of what to do in different circumstances.

- Model through example – catch yourself before you make a comment or vent about people or situations at school in front of the children.

Child Strategies

- Respect private conversations. If you notice two people seem to be having a personal talk (their voices are low and they are being private), give them some physical space and do not interrupt.

- Give your advice only when requested. If you hear someone sharing a problem, but they are not asking for your advice, they may not be open to or looking for someone's opinion.

- You do not have to fix it. When a peer or friend is having a problem (be it with a friend, a teacher, or parent) and you are not part of the problem, you do not have to fix it. The best thing you can do is be there to listen to your friend and be supportive, but don't add more "fuel to the fire" by getting involved.

- You can always ask. If you notice someone is crying or looks worried or confused, you may ask if he or she needs any help and respond based on their answer.

- Be cyber-courteous. If you are going to use a computer and find an email account open, sign the person out and do not look at their information.

- Respect people's property. Do not look in other people's things like desks, backpacks, room, diary, etc. without their permission.

Teacher's Guide to Social and Emotional Learning

- Respect privacy even if absent. If people are sharing information about someone else who is not there, say, "Maybe we should not talk about them since he/she is not here."

When you should intervene:

- If your friends are having problems and it is affecting you, you can try to help out by listening and sharing your thoughts.

- In dangerous situations – if you see two people physically fighting (even if you do not know them) or if someone is making risky choices, or if someone is hurt, it is helpful to let an adult know.

Parent Strategies

- Model with words – show your children how you respect others' privacy by being careful to not make judgmental comments about others' lives and decisions.

- Respect boundaries. Help your child have healthy boundaries by respecting their privacy; for instance, letting them have their diary, not eavesdropping on their conversations, and respecting their choices. Explain how with regard to technology and communication you need to be present and talk about how you can be involved based on your personal philosophy on this area.

- Teach children how to set boundaries. Practice ways in which they can ask someone to respect their boundaries, including family members, such as, "Can you please knock when you come in?" or "I need you to not grab my things or toys," or "I need for you to listen, but please do not tell me what to do."

- Help your child distinguish between meddling and helping.

- Don't jump to conclusions. Teach children that we do not always know the whole story of a situation and thus may not be able to formulate a judgment or opinion without having all the facts. For instance, if your child shares her teacher's response to something, before making a comment about how this was the wrong response, share that you may not know why she may have responded that way.

- Help build security and trust – children who feel confident and trust others will feel less need to get involved in social drama and gossip.

- Get your children to be active – kids who are busy and fulfilled have less time to worry or get involved in things that do not really concern them.

334

Discussion Topics

WHAT IS "MINDING MY OWN BUSINESS"?

"Minding your own business" is a phrase that refers to respecting the privacy of others. Sometimes the need to feel connected and natural curiosity lead people to question others when they feel that person knows interesting information; however, not all information is relevant to you. Minding your own business means recognizing that the information does not involve you and, out of respect, stopping yourself from asking about it.

SHOULD YOU ALWAYS MIND YOUR OWN BUSINESS?

In order to recognize a situation in which you should respect someone's privacy and one in which you can offer to help, you must pay close attention to the signals being given. Are the people involved speaking in low voices and making an effort not to be heard, showing that they do not wish to share their information, or does the person look lonely, as though they could use someone to talk to? It is also important to consider whether or not the people involved are in danger. Minding your own business does not mean ignoring someone who needs help.

Teacher's Guide to Social and Emotional Learning

DISCUSSION QUESTIONS

- Have you ever felt pressure from someone to share information that you didn't want to share? What did you say?

- When a friend shares a problem, should you offer your advice right away or wait to be asked?

- What should you say if your friends are gossiping about a situation that they are not involved in?

- What if you see someone doing something that does not involve you, but is against the rules?

Role Play

Scenario: Lamar heard someone tattling to the teacher on his best friend Victor.

Setting up the Scene: Please review the guidelines in the "How to use this book" section of the introduction.

Guided Questions: After the students have performed the scenario, ask the following questions *(invite both the actors and the rest of the class to answer)*:

DISCUSS FEELINGS:

- What is Lamar feeling?

- What is the boy who is tattling feeling?

   Teacher's Guide to Social and Emotional Learning

THINKING ABOUT CHOICES:

- What do you think could happen if Lamar warns Victor about what he heard?

- How would it benefit Lamar to warn Victor?

- What is the best thing for Lamar to do in a situation like this?

- Do you think it could become a habit for Lamar to get in the middle of things that don't concern him? What could happen if it becomes a habit?

338

MAKING IT PERSONAL:

Help students relate the scenario to their own lives by asking the following:

- Has a situation like this ever happened to you? What did you do?

- Is it easier to tell your friend that someone's tattling on them, or not say anything? Why?

- What kinds of things do you think or say to yourself to help you make a good choice and mind your own business?

- What are other situations similar to this where it was really hard to make a good choice (for example, knowing when to tell people that you heard others talking about them, and when to mind your own business)?

Refusal Skills

Children move through different stages of development, a path in which they are constantly forming their own identity by defining their boundaries and setting limits.

A Refusal Skill is when a person can clearly communicate that they do not want something or refuse to act a certain way. Behind the difficulty of saying "No" is often a deep-rooted fear of disappointing or letting someone down, a worry that someone will be mad, or a fear of being rejected and excluded. During childhood and the teenage years, making friends and fitting in are important aspects in a child's life and thus peer pressure can be stressful. Managing the need to be accepted and the necessity to become a separate individual is a delicate balancing act. This is why learning refusal skills – including both the verbal and body language versions – is an essential ability in that process of asserting oneself and being able to avoid risky behaviors, dangerous situations, and poor choices.

Teacher Strategies

- Teach a lesson on "refusal skills" in which children can practice the words and body language they could use in specific scenarios. Different "Refusal Skills Programs" are available that help guide children on how to say "No," offer alternative ways to say "No," be honest and assertive, use humor, and leave the situation when necessary.

- Create a safe place in which children can speak their mind, share their opinions, and can say "No" in an assertive and positive way.

- Talk to children about why they might want or need to say "No."

- Create activities for children to role-play and have the opportunity to understand the power of words and personal choice.

Child Strategies

- If something does not feel right, pause and think, "What could happen if I make this choice?"

- Use the word "No" and practice different ways you could say this, like, "No, that's not cool" or, "No, that is not a safe idea."

- If saying "No" does not work, change the topic (you can even make a joke), change who you are talking to, or change the location by leaving.

- Ask your parents about times when they have said "No" and what happened.

REFUSAL SKILLS

Parent Strategies

- Role play and practice with your child scenarios in which they can say "No" in an assertive tone and body language. Help them see the difference between a passive and an aggressive response vs. an assertive one.

- Allow for opportunities in which your child is able to make choices or say "No" to you.

- Come up with a code phrase with your child such as "Why is Aunt coming over?" which lets you know that they want to be picked up from a situation that makes them uncomfortable.

- Encourage your child to demonstrate assertiveness in different areas of their life.

Discussion Topics

WHAT IS A REFUSAL?

To refuse is to say "No." Saying "No" is sometimes harder than it sounds, particularly when saying "No" to a friend. Sometimes people have a hard time saying "No" to friends because they are worried that they will disappoint their friend or let them down. They worry that their friend will be angry and not like them anymore. This can cause them to say "yes," even if they are uncomfortable with the situation.

WHY SAY NO?

Even though it is hard, saying "No" is sometimes necessary in order to avoid making poor choices and getting into dangerous situations. By saying "No," you can become a role model for your friends and guide them toward the right choices.

DISCUSSION QUESTIONS

- Share a time when you said "No," even though it was difficult.

- Share a time when you did not say "No," but you wish that you had.

- What are some other ways to say "No"?

- What can you do if you say "No," but your friend does not listen?

- What should you do if a friend says "No" to you?

Role Play

Scenario: Alana is on a play date and her friend tells her she wants to show her a website that shows a shark attacking a swimmer.

Setting up the Scene: Please review the guidelines in the "How to use this book" section of the introduction.

Guided Questions: After the students have performed the scenario, ask the following questions *(invite both the actors and the rest of the class to answer)*:

DISCUSS FEELINGS:

- What is Alana feeling?

- What would Alana's parents feel if she visited this site?

THINKING ABOUT CHOICES:

- What do you think could happen if Alana checks out the site, since there is no way her parents will find out?

- How could Alana benefit from watching the video?

- What are some ways that Alana could say "No" to her friend?

- Do you think it could become a habit for Alana to participate in activities her parents would not want her to, just because she doesn't want to say "No"? What could happen if it becomes a habit?

348

MAKING IT PERSONAL:

Help students relate the scenario to their own lives by asking the following:

- Has a situation like this ever happened to you? What did you do?

- Is it easier to join your friend in doing something you are not supposed to do, or to refuse and tell them that it's a bad idea and suggest a different activity? Why?

- What kinds of things do you think or say to yourself to help you make a good choice and refuse to participate in activities which you know are not right?

- What are other situations similar to this where it was really hard to make a good choice (for example, when you had to say "No")?

Teacher's Guide to Social and Emotional Learning

Respecting Differences

We live in a world of diversity, be it in the variety of cultures, the presence of distinct religions, the array of languages, the differences in the way we learn and view the world, or the numerous customs and traditions that we follow. This is why it is crucial for our children not only to learn how to cope with diversity, but also to value and enrich their lives with understanding and embracing the similarities and differences around them. Teaching about diversity begins with recognizing that all people are unique in their own way and opening people up to the possibility of inclusiveness.

Respecting diversity can imply acknowledging differences in reading skills, athletic ability, cultural background, personality, religious beliefs, and the list goes on. As we recognize and are receptive of diversity, we grow in our ability to think about others, and we become flexible as we take different perspectives and develop our skills of compromise and respect.

Teacher Strategies

- Learn about your student's background, personality, interests, and learning style.

- Promote activities so that students learn about each other and appreciate the differences and similarities within the group.

- Create an environment where each student feels respected by addressing any putdowns, teasing, or negative comments about differences.

- Do a "rainbow of abilities" in which kids write down their personal array of strengths and areas of challenges. Have them share and think about how, when working in teams, they could use each other's strengths and support each other with their challenges.

- Have guest speakers on diversity, include class material which is inclusive, and use language that is respectful of differences.

Child Strategies

Take some time to reflect on what "Respecting Differences" means by doing the following:

- Think about how you are similar and different from friends or classmates.

- Thinking about your classmates, friends, and other kids that you know, do they speak different languages than you do or do they come from different countries or have a different religion? Do they look different? Do they have different abilities than you do (in math, reading, being social)?

- Why do you think it is important to respect differences?

- What could be challenging about having different backgrounds or beliefs?

Now that you took time to reflect, here are some things you can do:

- Show your interest in learning about different backgrounds and experiences.

- Be respectful when someone has a different way of learning or a different ability than you do.

- Remember the power of words: use kind and inclusive language.

- Treat others with respect and dignity.

Teacher's Guide to Social and Emotional Learning

Parent Strategies

So much of how our children understand and view diversity comes from home. Thus, it is important to:

- Begin by reflecting on what it means to you to raise a child in a diverse world. How do you understand and view diversity?

- Teach your child to be a critical thinker, by understanding and questioning the world around them with open hearts and open minds.

- Model respect, invite awareness, and incite interest about differences in the world (be it about religion, gender, age, abilities, cultures, ethnicity, etc.).

- Develop sensitivity in your children as you provide opportunities for them to be exposed to different realities by learning about other places and traditions, traveling if possible, and trying new things.

- Take a look at the possible stereotypes you may have and avoid making generalizations and negative comments about people (physical traits, abilities, background, color, gender, etc.).

- Share your own strengths/weaknesses and listen to your child's reflection on their own strengths and challenges accepting their own differences.

Discussion Topics

WHAT DOES IT MEAN TO RESPECT DIFFERENCES?

We live in a world of diversity with many different cultures, languages, and beliefs. Within your community, and even your family, there are things that make you different, as well as the same, as the people around you. Our differences make us who we are. They make us unique and special, and they make the world an interesting and exciting place to live. To show respect for people's differences means that you recognize and show consideration for the ways in which they are different from you.

WHY IS IT IMPORTANT TO RESPECT DIFFERENCES?

When you recognize and accept the characteristics and customs that make you different from others, you learn more about the people and places around you. You become more flexible in your thinking, and can therefore see things from a different perspective. This allows you to develop your ability to compromise and build successful relationships with the people you meet.

DISCUSSION QUESTIONS

- What is a characteristic or quality that makes you different from others?

- Share a time when you experienced an unfamiliar custom or tradition.

- Think about a friend or neighbor who comes from a different cultural background than you. What is something that makes you different? What is something that you have in common?

- What would the world be like if everyone was exactly the same?

- What is challenging about having different backgrounds and beliefs?

- What is exciting about having different backgrounds and beliefs?

Role Play

Scenario: Amelie is not very good at Four Square, but she would like to join a group of boys who are playing Four Square at recess.

Setting up the Scene: Please review the guidelines in the "How to use this book" section of the introduction.

Guided Questions: After the students have performed the scenario, ask the following questions *(invite both the actors and the rest of the class to answer)*:

DISCUSS FEELINGS:

- What is Amelie feeling?

- What are the boys who are playing Four Square feeling?

Teacher's Guide to Social and Emotional Learning

THINKING ABOUT CHOICES:

- What do you think could happen if the boys tell Amelie she is not that good at Four Square, and that they are an all-boys team?

- What could the boys gain by not allowing Amelie to join their game?

- What could the boys do to let Amelie join in?

- Do you think it could become a habit for the boys to avoid adding someone who is not that good to their team? What could happen if it becomes a habit?

MAKING IT PERSONAL:

Help students relate the scenario to their own lives by asking the following:

- Has a situation like this ever happened to you? What did you do?

- Is it easier to play with people who are more like you, or to teach others the rules of the game and let them join in? Why?

- What kinds of things do you think or say to yourself to help you make a good choice and be OK with being a little different?

- What are other situations similar to this where it was really hard to make a good choice (for example allowing new players into a game)?

Rumors, Gossip & Teasing

Words and actions are powerful. They can build, create, and shape, as well as hurt, offend, and damage. As children develop their connection and command of language and begin to manage their self-control, they experiment with the meaning of words and see how what they say or do may provoke different reactions and emotions in others and in themselves. They experiment and realize when having fun crosses the line and becomes hurtful teasing, such as when they make fun of the way someone looks or about their religion or abilities. This process is one of missteps and growth.

Rumors in particular can be very hurtful. In many ways, rumors spread as a way for individuals to feel part of a group or to get power or attention. There are also secondary gains in creating stories and relishing them with ill-fated details that are often not true. Many times children cannot gauge the reach of their words or actions, and, especially with technology, rumors and harsh language can be used behind the veils of anonymity.

Teacher's Guide to Social and Emotional Learning

Teacher Strategies

- Talk about the power of words and explore the wonderful opportunities language provides.

- Intervene when you hear a group of children using language to hurt others.

- Read books on gossip and role-play how to stop rumors by coaching and providing helpful language for kids to use.

- Guide the group to create guidelines and expectations on not spreading rumors.

- Help the children stop to think about the words that are inside their head before they say them out loud (as part of self-control).

- Play games, such as stating a variety of phrases and have kids analyze, compare, and contrast the body language, tone, and content in the message.

Child Strategies

- Don't spread the rumor – think about how the person may feel or be affected before you share information you heard with someone else. You may not have started the rumor, but you have the power to not spread it!

- To stop rumors, you can use phrases like, "We don't know if this is true" or, "Let's not talk about that person since they are not here," or just change the topic of conversation to avoid further rumors.

- Talk to your teacher if a rumor is spreading.

- If you see someone teasing someone else, stand up for that person (or for yourself, if you are the one being teased).

- Apologize if you hurt someone by teasing them, and avoid saying mean things to others.

- If you hear gossiping or are gossiping about someone else, think to yourself how that person would feel if they knew what you were saying. If they would not feel good, then you know that you are gossiping and it is best to change the topic.

Parent Strategies

- Pay attention to the words you use and how you speak of others in front of your child in order to model the behaviors you expect from your child.

- Notice and compliment your child when they use kind words.

- Intervene when you hear your child (or a group of his/her friends) use words in a negative, inappropriate, or demeaning way.

- Have fun with your child as you play with words and language.

- Teach your child to recognize body language and be congruent with the words they use.

- If a rumor has been spread about your child, talk to the teacher or school counselor to request their support and see if he/she can do an activity to address rumors and set clear boundaries for the children.

Discussion Topics

WHAT ARE RUMORS, GOSSIP, AND TEASING?

Words are powerful. They can inspire, encourage, and entertain. They can also hurt, offend, and damage. Gossip, rumors, and teasing are hurtful ways of speaking to and about others. Rumors are pieces of information or stories passed from one person to another without any proof that they are true. Similarly, gossip is the act of talking about someone when they are not there. Teasing is the act of making fun of or annoying someone in a mean way.

WHY DO PEOPLE ENGAGE IN RUMORS, GOSSIP, AND TEASING?

People engage in these harmful acts for many reasons, such as to feel like part of a group, to feel powerful, or to gain attention. Sometimes a person who engages in rumors, gossip, and teasing does not have a lot of confidence in themselves and tries to make themselves feel better by putting others down.

DISCUSSION QUESTIONS

- What can you say or do to stop a rumor from spreading?

- What can you say to someone who is gossiping about someone else?

- What can you do if you witness teasing?

- What advice would you give to a friend who is being teased?

- Who can you talk to if someone is spreading rumors or gossiping about you and will not stop?

- Social media sites like Facebook and methods like texting have provided new ways for people to tease others. Why do some people find it easier to tease others through social media and texting?

Role Play

Scenario: A group of girls tells Emma a rumor about her best friend Ava.

Setting up the Scene: Please review the guidelines in the "How to use this book" section of the introduction.

Guided Questions: After the students have performed the scenario, ask the following questions *(invite both the actors and the rest of the class to answer)*:

DISCUSS FEELINGS:

- What is Emma feeling?

- What is the group of girls feeling?

THINKING ABOUT CHOICES:

- What do you think could happen if Emma does not say anything bad about Ava, and remains quiet so that the girls don't say anything bad about her?

- What could Emma gain by not saying anything?

- What could Emma say to her friends to stop the rumor?

- Do you think it could become a habit for Emma to not say anything when she hears a rumor? What could happen if it becomes a habit?

MAKING IT PERSONAL:

Help students relate the scenario to their own lives by asking the following:

- Has a situation like this ever happened to you? What did you do?

- Is it easier to stand up for your friend and stop the rumor, or to not say anything? Why?

- What kinds of things do you think or say to yourself to help you make a good choice and avoid participating in gossiping or spreading rumors?

- What are other situations similar to this where it was really hard to make a good choice (for example, standing up for others, and reminding people that it's better not to gossip or spread rumors)?

Teacher's Guide to Social and Emotional Learning

Safety

Part of the wonder of childhood is having the ability to play, be curious, explore, and seek adventure. It is also a healthy and necessary part of child development in order to grow in confidence and independence, and build life skills. As children uncover and discover new experiences, they lead their parents through the exciting yet nerve-wracking process of finding a delicate balance between providing a sheltered environment while allowing room to fall, tumble, and hit some bumps on the road. Along the way, there are things parents can do to foster independence while helping children develop safety skills to ensure they avoid dangerous situations and make safe choices.

There are an array of topics that fall under the general umbrella of "Safety." From safety rules around the home, school or the playground, to precautions when participating in sports, to stranger-awareness, to safety online, it can be a humbling experience as caregivers to encounter our own vulnerability and the realization that we cannot control and protect children from many unwelcomed experiences. Adults can at times feel over-whelmed when addressing these issues, for instance in discussing sexual abuse prevention.

As caretakers, we can teach children to protect and care for themselves in their day-to-day lives. Just thinking about possible dangerous scenarios can make an adult, let alone a child, feel nervous and unprepared. However, being mindful of the child's age and making it an empowering learning experience for them can be a starting point when teaching safety skills. Talking about different situations is not enough (as it can raise anxiety if just discussed), but practicing tips, skills, and things to do or say in a variety of scenarios can be helpful and empowering.

Teacher Strategies

- Engage in safe sports – help athletes stay safe by encouraging parents to take their children to their physical exams, set aside time for warm-up, make sure kids are hydrated by establishing water breaks, teach them to wear the appropriate gear, and be knowledgeable of concussions or other injury signs or symptoms.

- Learn First Aid and CPR – attend trainings and review information regularly.

- Know your students. Be aware of any medical or health needs your students have, including allergies or diabetes.

- Practice drills. Know and practice the emergency plans, routes, and actions in case of a fire, earthquake, lockdown, etc.

- Teach about personal safety. In conjunction with administrators, review safety and abuse-prevention school programs to determine which one is best for your school setting.

- Provide parent education programs and resources.

- Read stories about safety. Depending on the safety topic you will be teaching (for instance, how to walk safely to and from school), find an age-appropriate story that can help introduce or reinforce the material you will be working on.

SAFETY

Teacher's Guide to Social and Emotional Learning

Child Strategies

- Follow the rules of safety. Rules usually have an important reason behind them and many are meant to keep you safe. Whether you are swimming in a pool or crossing a street, make sure you know what some of the basic rules are and stick to them. For instance, do not dive headfirst if the pool is shallow and don't run around the deck; be alert and look both ways when you cross a street.

- Wear the right gear. If you are riding a bike, skateboarding, or playing a sport, it is important you have the right equipment and wear it appropriately both during practice and games. You can avoid injuries with the right helmet, mouth guard, or lights and reflectors on your bicycle, etc.

- Take care of your body – listen to your body and give it what it needs. For instance, keep hydrated on a hot day or when playing sports, stretch if you will do some exercise, and eat healthy food.

- There is safety in numbers. Walk or go to places with friends. It is safer to be where there are other people close by to get help if you need it.

- Use your best judgment – if you feel unsure about a certain decision, talk to an adult first or look at what options feel safer.

Teacher's Guide to Social and Emotional Learning   374

Parent Strategies

- Have conversations with your children as to how to keep safe. For instance, talk about the rules in case of a fire, or your house rules about Internet safety or answering phone calls.

- Discuss the importance of rules. Explain the "Why?" behind guidelines as this will help your child understand the importance of rules and follow them.

- Children learn well when doing things, so help them practice how to put their gear on or role-play what they can and should not say when answering the phone.

- Introduce age-appropriate safety skills, and practice, review, and then build to a different skill. For instance, children younger than 10 have difficulty judging speed and distance, so they should not cross a street without an adult. However, they can still learn skills such as the importance of looking both ways before crossing, paying attention to sounds, making eye contact with the driver, etc. Similarly, before a child stays home alone, they should be emotionally and cognitively ready: they have to know how and when to call 911, know not to open the door to anyone or answer the phone, and how to distinguish an emergency from something that can wait, etc.

- Teach about personal safety. Talk to your children about their bodies and how to take care of their bodies in developmentally-appropriate ways.

SAFETY

Discussion Topics

WHAT IS SAFETY?

Being safe means staying away from situations that could cause you harm, knowing what to do if you find yourself in a dangerous situation, and taking positive actions that keep you physically and emotionally healthy.

WHY FOLLOW SAFETY RULES?

Rules usually have an important reason behind them and many are meant to keep you safe. Whether you are swimming in a pool or crossing a street, make sure you know the basic rules and stick to them, even if a friend is encouraging you to do otherwise. For instance, do not dive headfirst if the pool is shallow and don't run around the deck; be alert and look both ways when you cross a street. Your ability to follow rules shows the adults in your life that you are responsible enough to make some of your own decisions about keeping yourself safe.

376

DISCUSSION QUESTIONS

- Share some of the rules you follow at home.

- Share some of the rules you follow at school.

- Why do rules exist in sports like football or soccer, for example?

- Why is it important to practice safety drills for situations like fires and earthquakes?

- What can you say to a friend who is encouraging you to be unsafe?

- Have you ever experienced an unsafe situation with a friend? What did you say or do?

- What can you do if you see someone doing something unsafe?

Teacher's Guide to Social and Emotional Learning

Role Play

Scenario: Sam shows Derek a cool skateboard trick at the skate park. When Derek is trying the trick, he falls on his wrist and is unable to move.

Setting up the Scene: Please review the guidelines in the "How to use this book" section of the introduction.

Guided Questions: After the students have performed the scenario, ask the following questions *(invite both the actors and the rest of the class to answer)*:

DISCUSS FEELINGS:

- What is Sam feeling?

- What is Derek feeling?

THINKING ABOUT CHOICES:

- What do you think could happen if Sam tries to help his friend up and walk him home?

- How could Sam gain by trying to help Derek himself?

- What should Sam do to make the right choice in this situation?

- Do you think it could become a habit for Sam to try to deal with unsafe situations himself? What could happen if it becomes a habit?

MAKING IT PERSONAL:

Help students relate the scenario to their own lives by asking the following:

- Has a situation like this ever happened to you? What did you do?

- Is it easier to walk your friend home, or call your parents so they can take Derek to the doctor? Why?

- What kinds of things do you think or say to yourself to help you make good, safe choices?

- What are other situations similar to this where it was really hard to make a good choice (for example, when safety is an issue)?

Teacher's Guide to Social and Emotional Learning

Social Media Awareness

One of the most significant shifts in education today is the increased relevance and presence of technology. With this shift we realize that our guiding principles of learning still remain rooted in curiosity, creativity, communication, and collaboration.

It is a reality that with access to the Internet, students have the world at their fingertips. It is crucial for our schools and parents to help children build skills to adapt to this transition. For instance, parents need to help guide their children to navigate a wealth of information and unlimited access to constant social interaction. As overwhelming as this sometimes may sound or feel, parents can begin to do this by being actively involved in their child's life and becoming educated in ways children can use technology safely and effectively. On the other hand, schools need to create social media guidelines and policies to ensure children are using social media in a safe and appropriate way. Teachers and administrators need to understand ways students use social media to communicate, learn, and collaborate.

Teacher's Guide to Social and Emotional Learning

Teacher Strategies

- Have fun with technology while providing guidelines – technology offers such wonderful tools to enrich the curriculum. Explore ways in which your students can weave content and skills while using blogs, wikis, videos, digital stories or books, etc. It is crucial to set clear guidelines of expectations on language and content and to look for ways in which to monitor the content and protect who can access the information.

- Provide digital literacy. Offer technology awareness and education opportunities for students and parents through workshops, classes, or projects. Make sure it covers topics such as Internet safety, being a good cyber citizen, cyber bullying, and tips for children and parents.

- Follow an AUP. As a school, make sure you have an Acceptable User Policy (AUP). AUP is a set of rules created by the network manager to regulate and set the expectations for a healthy and positive use of technology.

- Facilitate dialogue with students and encourage them to think about and ask questions about what appropriate and inappropriate behavior looks like on social media, and what they should and should not use social media for.

- Implement social media into classroom activities and projects, and give children the option of doing assignments using social media or using traditional materials.

Child Strategies

To be a good cyber citizen, think about the following:

- Private info – don't give out your private information to anyone online, including full name, where you live, phone number, social security number, passwords, photos, or videos.

- A word on passwords – don't share your password with anyone, even friends. Passwords can only be shared with your parents.

- The golden rule – take care of other people's privacy by not sharing their photos, information, or videos without their permission.

- Watch your language – use kind and appropriate language as you communicate with friends, teachers, and others.

- Do not impersonate – do not lie and say you are someone else or create a false profile.

- Avoid cyber bullying – do not say anything mean or threatening to people online. If you see other people being mean, stand up for the victim. If you get any mean messages, do the following three things: do not respond, do not delete the message, and tell an adult.

SOCIAL MEDIA AWARENESS

Teacher's Guide to Social and Emotional Learning

Parent Strategies

- Become computer literate. Attend available workshops for parents in public libraries, schools, and other educational centers to learn the basic tips on Internet safety.

- Set behavioral rules around technology. It is important that you have continuous conversations with your child about your family's views and expectations about technology so that shared rules are discussed and revised as your children grow. This includes the expectations about what language, images, and content they can share online. Brainstorm the qualities of a good cyber citizen. Clarify that this includes their use of email, social networks, texts, apps, video games, etc.

- Create a space and time for devices. As a family, come up with the cyber rules of your home about spaces and times, for instance using computers in a common area, charging phones at night outside of the bedrooms, no texts before or after certain times, etc.

- Share an email account. For younger children, share an email account, guiding and modeling an appropriate use of this tool, and as they grow and have their own email account, agree as to how you will be able to monitor their communications based on your family's philosophy.

- Learn together. Accompany your child while using the

Internet and teach responsible online behavior (for example, practice writing emails to friends or teachers modeling the best language to use for each, take a look at websites you both like and set them as favorites, etc.).

- Teach Internet safety. Discuss the basic rules to stay safe on the Internet (not giving private information, not chatting with people they do not know, never meet alone in person with someone they met online, set boundaries of who it is OK to talk to and what topics are OK to discuss, etc.).

- Put parameters on online socializing. For young children, limit the websites your child can use to chat such as video games in which they can openly communicate with other people. Look for games that have established chat options the kids can choose from.

- Protect your child from cyber bullying. Teach your child the red flags of cyber bullying and what to do if they get a mean message (do not respond, show it to an adult, and save it as evidence).

Discussion Topics

WHAT IS SOCIAL MEDIA?

Social media is the sharing of information between friends and acquaintances through online communities and networks such as Snapchat, Instagram, and Twitter. Using social media has become a widely accepted form of communication.

WHAT DOES IT MEAN TO BE A GOOD CYBER CITIZEN?

A good cyber citizen is someone who uses technology and social media in a responsible way. Good cyber citizens are careful not to share too much personal information, are respectful of other people's information and do not share things like photos or video without permission, use appropriate language, and do not pretend to be someone that they are not. Good cyber citizens do not participate in cyber bullying.

DISCUSSION QUESTIONS

- What kind of social media do you participate in?

- Share some of the rules you follow when using social media.

- Do you think social media contributes positively to relationships? Why or why not?

- Share a negative experience you had with social media.

- What would you do if someone asked for your personal information while you were online?

- What would you do if you saw a negative post about you on a social media site?

- What would you say or do if your friend wanted you to help him/her create a fake Facebook page?

Role Play

Scenario: Kayla finds out via a group email picture that her good friend Rose had a birthday party and she was not invited.

Setting up the Scene: Please review the guidelines in the "How to use this book" section of the introduction.

Guided Questions: After the students have performed the scenario, ask the following questions (*invite both the actors and the rest of the class to answer*):

DISCUSS FEELINGS:

- What is Kayla feeling?

- What is Rose feeling?

THINKING ABOUT CHOICES:

- What do you think could happen if Kayla makes a mean comment on Rose's email?

- What could Kayla gain by not hanging out with Rose from now on?

- What could Kayla say to Rose about how she feels?

- Do you think it could become a habit for Kayla to make mean comments on the Internet when she's upset? What could happen if it becomes a habit?

388

MAKING IT PERSONAL:

Help students relate the scenario to their own lives by asking the following:

- Has a situation like this ever happened to you? What did you do?

- Is it easier to make a mean comment on social media, or to talk to your friend in person about your feelings? Why?

- What kinds of things do you think or say to yourself to help you make good choices and avoid sharing rude or inappropriate things on social media?

- What are other situations similar to this where it was really hard to make a good choice (for example, saying things on social media when you're upset or angry)?

Stranger Awareness

Personal safety and how to set healthy personal boundaries are essential skills to teach children. However, discussing these topics can sometimes make a child (or even an adult) feel anxious or fearful. Thus, it can be helpful to introduce this topic by focusing on safety rules and awareness and helping children practice or role-play ways to be assertive.

We know that there are different risks that a child could encounter and we want to make sure they are safe when with strangers, for example. As we talk to children, a useful perspective is to talk about "Stranger Safety" rather than "Stranger Danger." Safety rules can be discussed and practiced to help the child be more aware both in new surroundings with strangers, as well as with adults that they do know. It is important to keep in mind that statistics show us that it is more likely for a child to be harmed by someone they know than by a stranger. This is why it is very important to discuss stranger awareness as well as how to set healthy boundaries with people they know.

 Teacher's Guide to Social and Emotional Learning

Teacher Strategies

- Explore, in conjunction with administrators, safety and abuse prevention school programs to determine which one is best for your school setting.

- Provide parent education programs and resources.

- Teach children to not go anywhere with someone they don't know.

- Read stories on the topic to children.

- Teach assertive communication skills (tone, body language, eye contact).

Child Strategies

Know that:
- Most people, including strangers, are good.

- A stranger is just someone you don't know and he or she can look like anybody.

- When you are with strangers or on your own, it is important to follow safety rules to take care of yourself.

If you are on your own (even for a little while), be more aware of your surroundings and follow the safety rules below:
- Walk or go to places with friends. It is safer to be where there are other people close by to get help if you need it.

- Do not give personal information to a stranger or to someone who makes you feel uncomfortable.

- It is OK to get help from strangers if there is an emergency.

- Keep a safe distance or walk away from a stranger if they try to approach you or offer you something.

- Your voice is powerful – if you are alone and approached by a stranger who gets too close, hold up both hands and say, "STOP" in a loud voice. If they try to grab you, yell, "HELP! I do not know this person."

- Talk to your parents about your family's rules answering the door, being on the phone, and being on the Internet.

Parent Strategies

- Share in a calm way that you believe most people are good, but there are a few people who have problems and may hurt kids. As a result, it is important to follow safety rules when with strangers and "Stranger Safety" (being with friends, telling an adult who is caring for them if they will go somewhere, learning how to take care of their personal space, what words to use if someone approaches them, etc.) will help them do so.

- Read simple books to help your child understand that their body belongs to them.

- Teach them that touch for play, teasing, or affection has to be both people's choice and it has to be safe.

- Clarify that no one should touch his/her private areas (the parts of the body covered by a bathing suit) unless it is a doctor in case of a health situation.

- No one should ask him/her to touch them in their private areas.

- Touch or other behavior that bothers them should never have to be a secret.

- Help them practice how to clearly say "No" to unwanted or inappropriate behaviors using eye contact and assertive body language.

- Ask your children, "Is there anything you've been wondering or worrying about that you haven't told me?" and listen to their answers with patience.

394

Discussion Topics

WHAT IS A STRANGER?

A stranger is a person that you do not know, and he or she can look like anybody. The world is a great big place, and we are surrounded by people we do not know all the time. When you are with strangers or on your own, it is important to follow safety rules to take care of yourself. If you are on your own, even for a little while, be more aware of your surroundings and follow safety rules like making sure to walk places with friends and never taking anything from someone you do not know.

ARE ALL STRANGERS BAD?

No. The truth is most strangers are good. They are only a stranger because you have never met them. However, because you have never met them, and do not know how they treat other people, it is important to keep your distance.

DISCUSSION QUESTIONS

- Should you ever give your personal information to someone that you do not know? Why or why not?

- Is it OK to accept help from someone you do not know if you are having an emergency? What is an example of this?

- What should you do if a stranger asks you to come with them?

- What can you say to a stranger who is trying to talk to you?

- What kind of rules do you follow at home about answering the door or the phone?

- What should you do if you would like to talk with someone but you have never met them before?

Role Play

Scenario: Chelsea is walking home alone from school when she notices a car slowing down. The driver asks her for directions to school.

Setting up the Scene: Please review the guidelines in the "How to use this book" section of the introduction.

Guided Questions: After the students have performed the scenario, ask the following questions *(invite both the actors and the rest of the class to answer)*:

DISCUSS FEELINGS:

- What is Chelsea feeling?

- What would Chelsea's parent feel if Chelsea talked to the stranger?

THINKING ABOUT CHOICES:

- What do you think could happen if Chelsea politely goes up to the car and gives the driver directions?

- What could Chelsea gain by talking to the stranger?

- What should Chelsea do when the driver talks to her?

- Do you think it could become a habit for Chelsea to speak with strangers to be polite? What could happen if it becomes a habit?

MAKING IT PERSONAL:

Help students relate the scenario to their own lives by asking the following:

- Has a situation like this ever happened to you? What did you do?

- Is it easier to answer a stranger's question, or ignore them and go to your house (or a friend's house if it's closer) in a situation like this? Why?

- What kinds of things do you think or say to yourself to help you make good choices and avoid talking to strangers?

- What are other situations similar to this where it was really hard to make a good choice (for example, when strangers are involved)?

Teacher's Guide to Social and Emotional Learning

Organization Skills

Planning

As new technology and research help us understand further how the brain works, the relevance of executive functions have risen to the forefront. Executive functions refer to a group of mental skills mainly coordinated by the frontal lobe (Alvarez, J. A. & Emory, E., Julie A.; Emory, Eugene, 2006). These cognitive abilities include organization and planning, attention, time management, memory, and regulation.

Children benefit from developing and ensuring sound executive skills such as organizational, planning, and studying abilities, which will serve as life skills in school, work, and relationships. However, this is a process of learning that requires teaching systems, strategies, and tools, and modeling good habits. Even then, for some children executive functions may be a challenge and they may need further support. Early interventions can prove to be beneficial as the brain is malleable and is shaped both by physical changes as well as by ongoing experiences.

Teacher Strategies

- Write down homework and project dates on the board.

- Provide visual organizers.

- Break down larger projects into smaller steps.

- Introduce checklists and completion lists on projects.

- Remind children to clean their desks and area of work.

- Review calendar dates and daily routines.

- Use color codes as a way to categorize or organize materials.

- Organize book bag clean-ups.

Child Strategies

- Get your things ready for school the night before.

- Organize your workspace (your desk at school and at home).

- Make a checklist with words or drawings of things to do. This list can be a sticky note in a notebook for school work, or a list stuck on the refrigerator for house chores.

- Clean up your backpack and organize your papers.

- Write things in a calendar or school planner.

- Make flash cards to help you study or organize ideas.

- Ask for help if you are having a hard time getting organized.

PLANNING

Parent Strategies

- Help instill sound habits by teaching your child from an early age to clean up his/her room.

- Make it your child's habit to get ready the night before.

- Set a homework time and space.

- Assign chores that are age-appropriate.

- Keep a family calendar to help visualize events and planning.

- Help create simple checklists like "things to get ready in the morning" or "three things to do before going to sleep."

- Guide your child in how to plan for their homework and create a routine.

Discussion Topics

WHAT IS PLANNING?

Planning is the act of figuring out how to accomplish something ahead of time. Planning is a life skill that plays an important role at school, work, and in relationships. There are many strategies and tools that can be used to help you plan and therefore successfully accomplish your tasks.

WHY PLAN AHEAD?

Planning ahead helps you to complete your tasks in an organized manner and to the best of your abilities. Rather than scrambling to take care of your responsibilities, planning ahead ensures that you have the resources and time you need to do your best work.

Teacher's Guide to Social and Emotional Learning

DISCUSSION QUESTIONS

- What are some tasks that you regularly plan ahead for?

- What kinds of tools do you use to plan ahead?

- Share some planning techniques that you use at home.

- Share some planning techniques that you use at school.

- Do the adults in your life plan ahead? What are some examples of this?

- Share a time when you did not plan ahead and had to face challenging consequences.

Role Play

Scenario: Cheng just woke up late and he realizes that he needs to get his backpack ready for school.

Setting up the Scene: Please review the guidelines in the "How to use this book" section of the introduction.

Guided Questions: After the students have performed the scenario, ask the following questions *(invite both the actors and the rest of the class to answer)*:

DISCUSS FEELINGS:

- What is Cheng feeling?

- What are Cheng's parents feeling?

Teacher's Guide to Social and Emotional Learning

THINKING ABOUT CHOICES:

- What do you think could happen if Cheng continues to wake up late and does not get his backpack ready the night before?

- What could Cheng gain by leaving things to the last minute?

- How could Cheng plan ahead so that he is not rushed in the morning?

- Do you think it could become a habit for Cheng to not plan ahead? What could happen if this becomes a habit?

410

MAKING IT PERSONAL:

Help students relate the scenario to their own lives by asking the following:

- Has a situation like this ever happened to you? What did you do?

- Is it easier to get your backpack ready in the morning, or plan ahead and do things the night before? Why?

- What kinds of things do you think or say to yourself to help you make a good choice and plan ahead?

- What are other situations similar to this where it was really hard to make a good choice (for example, when you have to plan ahead)?

PLANNING

Teacher's Guide to Social and Emotional Learning

Setting Goals

Many of us have experienced the subtle pleasure that comes from checking a box off our "to-do list," especially if we know that this is one small step taking us closer to perhaps a greater goal which we are working towards achieving.

Ideally, we begin to acquire the building blocks of goal-setting when we are children, be it that we decide to save some money to buy something special, get involved in gymnastics, or decide to learn to play an instrument. The ingredients we need to achieve our objectives include being able to have a vision or a dream which is often closely related to a passion; having the ability to discern a target and the steps to reach it; having the discipline and resilience to go through different strides; and having the right blend of hope, confidence, and perseverance. Parents play an instrumental role in this journey, as they provide the desirable balance of having expectations and aspirations for their child, while providing the unwavering belief and confidence in their child's ability to eventually achieve their best.

Teacher Strategies

Provide your students with opportunities to set and reach goals. Depending on time and possibilities, craft different options in which kids can set targets and work to reach them. This can take the shape of a shared class project (like building something together) or an individual goal in which kids write down their expectations, dreams and hopes for reading, writing, or doing specific projects.

- Break down into steps. Have students fill out charts or visual organizers that help them learn the steps of setting goals, making a plan, defining responsibilities, and assessing progress within a timeline.

- Make time for reflection and celebration. Teach kids to focus on the process by providing guiding questions on how they reached certain goals, how it felt to not meet their goals the first time, what they learned, what feelings come from reaching a goal, etc.

414

Child Strategies

- Create a vision. Think of something you would like to accomplish, like making one basket in a basketball game, or reading a certain number of books during the summer. Make an image in your mind of yourself doing it: how do you look? What do you think you might be feeling? Who is sharing the moment with you?

- Draw it or write it down. Make a drawing or write your goal on a piece of paper. You can post it somewhere or share it with your parents or friends.

- Be specific. Try to make your goal specific and reachable. Your parents or teachers can help with this by asking you questions and helping define it.

- Plan steps. Write down steps you need to take to reach your goal and consider the following W's. For the example below, let's imagine you want to save money for a toy you like, and you decide to have a garage sale:

  - What – Think of what you will need to make your plan work, such as the materials you might need. You will need to collect things you can sell during the garage sale and can ask friends to donate stuff.

Teacher's Guide to Social and Emotional Learning

- When and Where – Ask yourself if you need a place for your plan to be successful, and set timelines of when you will do what is needed. You will sell the items you gather at your aunt's home since it is ideal for garage sales, and it will be on a designated Saturday from 10 to 1.

- Who – Decide who is responsible for the different steps. You will find the things to sell, ask your aunt for permission, make posters, and get help from your parents with taking the things in their car.

• Assess. Think of how your plan is working out and if you need to make any changes. Perhaps you find out it may rain on the day you had planned the garage sale, so you might need to postpone the date.

• Celebrate. Celebrate your effort, mistakes, and successes. Remember you will learn from the whole experience (the ups and downs) and feel proud of what you accomplish.

Parent Strategies

- Share your passion and journeys. Sharing with your child your own stories on how you have reached your goals is a wonderful way to build their trust and outlook on achieving a goal.

- Help them find their own calling. Explore with your child what some of their passions are, as well as their interests and curiosities, so that you can help guide them to define a goal. You can provide some suggestions, but follow their lead.

- Start small and be specific. Children do best starting with short-term, achievable goals that they can reach with effort but which are also manageable. Together, come up with a fun and clear goal he can set, for instance finishing a book or an art project.

- Design a path. Help your child make a plan and think of small steps that can help keep motivation high and give the process direction. For instance, if your child decides to create a vegetable garden, help come up with a list of things that need to be bought, where the garden would be, a chart to remember when to water the garden, etc. You can help set a structure by coming up with charts or visual aids to help designate the who, when, what, and where.

- Balance realism and magical thinking – help your child

have the right balance of magical thinking while providing a reality check. Children can get easily frustrated once they hit their first challenge or suddenly feel overwhelmed with a daunting project. Parents can encourage their children and be supportive, while still pointing out some of the difficulties that they may find along the way. For instance, in foreseeing some of the problems that may arise, parents can help children problem-solve with anticipation and come up with strategies to face possible challenges.

• Celebrate mistakes and successes – Let your child know that the process is as important as or possibly more important than the end product. Celebrate with your child the learning that comes from making mistakes and be there to support them during the disappointments. Recognize your child's grit and perseverance when reaching the goal. Give compliments on each of the steps reached, and provide time for reflection on the process.

418

Discussion Topics

WHAT IS A GOAL?

A goal is a result or end product that someone wants and works toward. Reaching a goal gives people a feeling of fulfillment and satisfaction, especially when they know that they have given their best, have persevered, and feel proud of the outcome.

WHY ARE GOALS IMPORTANT?

The ability to set goals is a life skill that works hand-in-hand with planning and time management. Having clear goals enables people to think through the steps they need to take to accomplish the task they have set themselves. While planning and time management help people fulfill their responsibilities, working toward a goal tends to be more personal. Goals are often related to skills people wish to acquire or the completion of a task that they care a lot about. Achieving a goal can result in a great sense of accomplishment and pride.

Teacher's Guide to Social and Emotional Learning

DISCUSSION QUESTIONS

- Share a time when you worked hard and accomplished a goal.

- Share a goal that you are working toward right now.

- What obstacles do people face when working toward their goals?

- If a goal takes a long time to reach, should you give up? Why or why not?

- What goal are you most proud of accomplishing?

- What advice would you give to a friend who wants to give up on their goal?

- What tools can you use to accomplish your goals?

- How can you use planning and time management to achieve your goals?

Role Play

Scenario: Adriana's mom has asked her to clean up her closet by the end of the day. She is halfway done and feels too bored to complete it.

Setting up the Scene: Please review the guidelines in the "How to use this book" section of the introduction.

Guided Questions: After the students have performed the scenario, ask the following questions *(invite both the actors and the rest of the class to answer)*:

DISCUSS FEELINGS:

- What is Adriana feeling?

- What is Adriana's mom feeling?

SETTING GOALS

Teacher's Guide to Social and Emotional Learning

THINKING ABOUT CHOICES:

- What do you think could happen if Adriana takes a break and tells her mom she will do it another day?

- What could Adriana gain by dumping everything into a box and saying it is done?

- What could Adriana do to complete the job today?

- Do you think it could become a habit for Adriana to avoid finishing tasks when she gets bored? What could happen if it becomes a habit?

MAKING IT PERSONAL:

Help students relate the scenario to their own lives by asking the following:

- Has a situation like this ever happened to you? What did you do?

- Is it easier to avoid completing the job, or to divide the work into smaller pieces and give yourself little rewards for completing each part of the job? Why?

- What kinds of things do you think or say to yourself to help you make good choices and set goals?

- What are other situations similar to this where it was really hard to make a good choice (for example, setting goals at school or at home so you do a good job)?

Time Management

Organization, prioritization, and time management are valuable skills for academic and personal success. Creating healthy learning and organizational habits can start at an early age by helping a child establish routines and set appropriate systems in place that support his or her specific learning style, strengths, and needs. Establishing general guidelines of when and where to do homework will help set sound study habits and is a good starting point. In addition, knowing the child's main learning style can help determine specific strategies to support him or her further. There are three main learning styles: visual, auditory, and kinesthetic (Walter Burke Barbe; Raymond H. Swassing; Michael N. Milone, Jr., June 1979). Although everyone uses these three venues to learn and has a combination of these learning styles, one way may be the preferred mode to acquire information.

A child who is mainly a visual learner can benefit from looking at graphic organizers, color-coding materials, making flashcards, watching a demonstration, or reading. For an auditory learner, the child may learn best by reciting information, taping the information and listening to it, doing oral presentations, or having music or a noise-cancellation device when studying. Kinesthetic learners prefer a "hands-on" method and will learn best by doing things, thus they may need to study or work while pacing, write notes (even if they do not use them afterwards), spell words in the air, doodle while studying, or create projects and draw pictures of the content.

Knowing what works best for the student (which can be very different from what works for his or her parents) can help determine what may be the best strategies to put in place. Some children may need more support than others, and it may take some trial and error to find what suits them best. Technology now offers some helpful apps that create "to-do" lists, graphic organizers, electronic binders and calendars, etc. Although these are useful tools for all, these options can be particularly helpful for students with specific learning needs. Working closely with an educator or a learning specialist can be valuable in order to help the child determine the strategies that work best for them and teaches them to be self-advocates of their own learning.

Teacher Strategies

- Get to know what type of learners your students are and provide opportunities that offer visual, auditory, and kinesthetic modes of learning for all.

- Make mind maps, visual organizers, outlines, graphs, and charts, and put instructions on the board (visual).

- Take fieldtrips, integrate material with projects (art, robotics, and gardening), have students do observations and report back in different formats, and integrate dance, music, and movement into an activity (kinesthetic).

- Read aloud or listen to audio books, have students do oral presentations, have a quiet time and a music time, and give verbal instructions (auditory).

- Create a daily routine within your class in which you model and help students get organized by reviewing the daily planner, thinking about how long a certain project might take, color coding or writing notes about upcoming projects or quizzes, cleaning backpacks and desks, and arranging papers into folders.

- Explore the possibility of giving a study skills workshop that covers topics such as how to take notes, studying techniques, mindfulness, and prioritization.

Teacher's Guide to Social and Emotional Learning

Child Strategies

- Use a daily planner. Schools will usually give you a planner or you can get one yourself; talk to your parents to see if having an electronic planner might work for you.

- Use to-do lists. Create your own to-do lists by writing down what you need to work on and have a blank box next to each item so you can check it off when it is done.

- Prioritize assignments. Before sitting down to do your homework, make a list of assignments and write a number next to each one in the order you will complete them. Do a simple and quick piece of homework first, and then plan to do the longer and harder one somewhere in the middle of your list.

- Estimate the time – think about approximately how long each assignment will take and write it down in your list. You can use a kitchen timer to set the time and try to do it in the timeframe that you planned. You sometimes might go over or finish before and that's OK; with practice, you will start figuring out how much time you usually need for each assignment.

- Create a binder. Use a binder to assign a section of work "To turn in" and work "To do."

- Have a weekly clean up – clean up your backpack once a week and review paperwork so that it is not as heavy and stays organized.

Parent Strategies

Organization and Time Management

- Set a daily study place and time. Find a spot in which your child can work quietly and can spread her materials out; it should also be a place in which you can be accessible to provide help if needed. Find a designated time that works best with your child's schedule and which is consistent. After school, provide some down-time, rest, and a snack before starting with homework.

- Keep a household calendar, and in it include family commitments as well as major projects or tests to help plan accordingly.

- Work with your child to plan long-term projects by breaking them up into smaller chunks with frequent deadlines. Create a timeline that shows the progress.

- Help your child create a binder with different tabs as needed ("To turn in" and "To do," or based on classes). You might need to help supervise this initially and then on and off as they become better at using it on their own.

Studying and Reviewing

- Help your child make a plan as to when they should start studying for a quiz or test, allowing for enough time to be prepared.

- Show him how to highlight text and take notes when reading. For instance, with yellow highlight the main idea of a paragraph, with orange highlight the supporting details, and with green, mark words he does not know; he should highlight key words and not full sentences.

- Have her summarize what she just read or the concept studied using her own words.

- Help your child study using different modes (reading out loud, acting out a concept, drawing symbols for words or ideas, creating a presentation, using flash cards, teaching the information to you, etc.).

Homework

- Help him set a routine before starting with homework by going over his planner, and making a list of priorities and times for each assignment. As your child progresses in this skill, allow him to become more independent while still being there for supervision as needed. Some children may need more support in this area, especially in the beginning of each school year when expectation of homework changes.

- When your child needs help with homework, ask questions that help her break down the problem into smaller steps. Help your child identify patterns, ideas, and information to develop problem-solving skills.

Discussion Topics

WHAT IS TIME MANAGEMENT?

Time management is an organizational skill that refers specifically to how you organize the time you have been given to accomplish a task. Learning to use your time wisely is a skill that will serve you throughout your life.

WHY DO YOU NEED TO MANAGE YOUR TIME?

Establishing a routine and timetable for how you fulfill your responsibilities is important for future success. For example, following a set routine for when and where you do your homework helps you to develop good study habits. There are many tools available to help you manage and track your time; for example, using daily planners.

Teacher's Guide to Social and Emotional Learning

DISCUSSION QUESTIONS

• What tools do you use to help manage your time?

• How can using a "to-do" list help you accomplish your tasks?

• Do you do your homework at the same time every day? Why or why not?

• Do you do your homework in a certain order? Why or why not?

• Share a routine that you complete on a daily basis.

• Share a time when you did not manage your time well. What was the consequence?

Role Play

Scenario: Calvin has just completed a big social studies project that he will turn in tomorrow. Part of his grade depends on the presentation he will give to the class when he turns it in.

Setting up the Scene: Please review the guidelines in the "How to use this book" section of the introduction.

Guided Questions: After the students have performed the scenario, ask the following questions *(invite both the actors and the rest of the class to answer)*:

DISCUSS FEELINGS:

- What is Calvin feeling?

- What are Calvin's parents feeling about the presentation?

TIME MANAGEMENT

THINKING ABOUT CHOICES:

- What do you think could happen if Calvin packs the project into his backpack and watches TV, since he can always wing the presentation?

- What could Calvin gain by watching TV instead of practicing his presentation?

- What are some ways that Calvin could use his time wisely to prepare for his presentation?

- Do you think it could become a habit for Calvin to not build his time management and organizational skills? If it becomes a habit, what could happen?